HOW TO READ F1

JENNIE GOW

BOOKS

BBC Books, an imprint of Ebury Publishing
Penguin Random House UK
One Embassy Gardens, 8 Viaduct Gdns,
Nine Elms, London SW11 7BW

BBC Books is part of the Penguin Random House group of companies
whose addresses can be found at global.penguinrandomhouse.com

Copyright © Jennie Gow 2024

Illustrations © Jack Smyth

Jennie Gow has asserted her right to be identified as the author of this Work
in accordance with the Copyright, Designs and Patents Act 1988

Penguin Random House values and supports copyright. Copyright fuels creativity, encourages diverse voices, promotes freedom of expression and supports a vibrant culture. Thank you for purchasing an authorised edition of this book and for respecting intellectual property laws by not reproducing, scanning or distributing any part of it by any means without permission. You are supporting authors and enabling Penguin Random House to continue to publish books for everyone. No part of this book may be used or reproduced in any manner for the purpose of training artificial intelligence technologies or systems. In accordance with Article 4(3) of the DSM Directive 2019/790, Penguin Random House expressly reserves this work from the text and data mining exception.

This book is unofficial and is not associated in any way with the Formula 1 companies.
F1, FORMULA ONE, FORMULA 1, FIA FORMULA ONE WORLD CHAMPIONSHIP,
GRAND PRIX and related marks are trade marks of Formula One Licensing B.V.

First published by BBC Books in 2024

www.penguin.co.uk

A CIP catalogue record for this book is available from the British Library

ISBN 9781785949241

Printed and bound in Great Britain by Clays Ltd, Elcograf S.p.A.

The authorised representative in the EEA is Penguin Random House Ireland,
Morrison Chambers, 32 Nassau Street, Dublin D02 YH68.

Penguin Random House is committed to a sustainable future for our business, our readers and our planet. This book is made from Forest Stewardship Council® certified paper.

For Jamie and Izzy

CONTENTS

F1 in Numbers   1

Introduction   2

A is for ... Aero, Alex Albon, Fernando Alonso, Alpine, Apex, Aston Martin and Australia   5

B is for ... Oliver Bearman, Valtteri Bottas, Braking, Ross Brawn, Broadcasting and Jenson Button   13

C is for ... Calendar, CFD, Champagne, Chassis, Cockpit, Constructors' Championship, Contracts, David Coulthard, Crashes and Crowd   23

D is for ... Degradation, Delta, Diffuser, Stefano Domenicali, Donuts, Downforce, *Drive to Survive* and DRS   35

E is for ... Bernie Ecclestone, Engineers and Engines   43

F is for ... Father/Son, Ferrari, FIA, Flags, Flat-Spot, Formation Lap and the 'F' Word (F-Duct)   49

G is for ... Garages, Pierre Gasly, GOATs, Grid, Grid Walks, Grand Chelem, Grand Prix and Gravel   59

H is for ... Haas, Halo, Lewis Hamilton, Helmets,   **69**
Christian Horner, Nico Hulkenberg, James Hunt
and Hydraulics

I is for ... Innovation   **83**

J is for ... Japan, Jump Start and Junior Categories   **87**

K is for ... Karting and KERS   **91**

L is for ... Laps, Niki Lauda, Charles Leclerc, Lights Out   **95**
and Lella Lombardi

M is for ... Kevin Magnussen, Marbles, Marshals,   **101**
McLaren, Mechanics, Media, Mercedes, Monaco
and Money

N is for ... Adrian Newey, Nomex, Lando Norris   **113**
and Nuts

O is for ... Esteban Ocon, Oversteer/Understeer   **121**
and Overtaking

P is for ... Paddock, Parc Fermé, Sergio Pérez,   **125**
Oscar Piastri, Pits, Pit Board, Pit Stops, Plank,
Podium, Points, Pole Position and Alain Prost

Q is for ... Qualifying   **137**

R is for ... Race Director, Rain, Records, Red Bull,   **139**
Retirements, Daniel Ricciardo, Ride Height, Rivals,
Nico Rosberg and George Russell

S is for ... Carlos Sainz, Logan Sargeant, Sauber,   **157**
Michael Schumacher, Sectors, Ayrton Senna,
Silverstone, SIMs, Guenther Steiner, Stewards,
Sir Jackie Stewart, Strategy and Lance Stroll

T is for ... Tear-off Strip, Telemetry, Timing, Jean Todt,   **175**
Yuki Tsunoda and Tyres

U is for ... United States and Unsafe Release   **181**

V is for ... Max Verstappen and Sebastian Vettel   **185**

W is for ... Williams, Susie Wolff, Toto Wolff, Women   **193**
and World Champions

X is for ... X-Wing   **203**

Y is for ... Yachts   **205**

Z is for ... Zhou Guanyu   **209**

References   **211**

Acknowledgements   **213**

About the Author   **215**

F1 IN NUMBERS

1 The number usually on the car of the current World Champion (not always – Lewis Hamilton chose to retain number 44 when he was champion).

2 Number of women who have started an F1 race (Maria Teresa de Filippis and Lella Lombardi).

5 Nigel Mansell and Sebastian Vettel both carried this number on their car; other than the defending champion's number 1 it has won the most Drivers' Championships.

10 Number of teams competing in F1 each year.

17 The car number retired by the FIA after Jules Bianchi died in 2015.

25 Number of points awarded for winning a Grand Prix.

34 Number of drivers who have won a World Championship.

41 Number of nations that have been represented in F1.

107 In the first part of qualifying, a driver must set a lap time within 107 per cent of the fastest Q1 time or must appeal to the stewards that they are fast enough to race safely.

776 Number of drivers who have raced in F1 from when it began in 1950 up to 2023.

4,000 Average number of personnel on the ground for an F1 race.

INTRODUCTION

I love F1.

It's the pinnacle of motorsport. The perfect blend of human and machine. F1 cars race around the world's best tracks reaching speeds of over 230mph (370kph).

I first stepped into the F1 paddock in Canada 2011, filling in as BBC Radio 5 Live's pit-lane reporter. A monumental downpour saw the much-interrupted race last over four hours; it turned out to be longest race in Formula One history. It was thrilling and I was immediately drawn to the excitement and drama of F1.

Since then, I have covered over 200 races for the BBC as their F1 presenter and pit-lane reporter. I've seen four different drivers claim World Championship titles, been drenched and sunburnt as I've roamed the paddocks and pit lanes of the world, and followed the most amazing, fast-paced, high-tech, action-packed, politically charged, life-and-death moments of the best sport in the world.

There may only be 20 drivers fighting for the F1 title, but actually it's a team sport with thousands of people (and millions of pounds) being spent on Formula One.

Since the inception of the ground-breaking Netflix documentary series *Drive to Survive* (which I was proud to be invited to be part of from season three onwards) the

Introduction

popularity of F1 has grown exponentially, with new fans flocking to the sport.

In 2022, I suffered a major stroke and as part of my rehabilitation (while missing being in the paddock terribly) I decided to write this book as a way of sharing my experiences and knowledge of F1. So, whether you're a new fan, have followed the sport for years, or just want to know what all the fuss is about, this is for you!

As I say, I love F1, and I love sharing my passion. Hopefully, by the end of this book (if you didn't already) you will love Formula One too.

A is for
AERO, ALEX ALBON, FERNANDO ALONSO, ALPINE, APEX, ASTON MARTIN and **AUSTRALIA**

AERO

Aero – or aerodynamics – is the study of motion and air; in other words, how the air moves when an F1 car drives through it.

We could get really bogged down in this subject. A vast amount of time and millions of pounds are spent by teams designing the best aerodynamics for their car. It's a compromise between downforce and drag – aiming to be fast both on the straights and in the corners. The sleek lines of an F1 car today look very different to the beautiful but clunky-looking cars of the 1950s and 60s, a development that tells the story of aero. The fastest cars have the best aero packages – the 2023 Red Bull (designed by Adrian Newey and his team) had an aerodynamic design that was practically unbeatable. The way the air works with the car, and flows around the car, is like a hot knife cutting through butter. If you want to know more about 'Aero', I suggest you read Adrian Newey's book, *How to Build a Car*.

ALEX ALBON

Alex races under the Thai flag although he is part British and has lived in the UK for most of his life. Resilience should be his middle name. He became part of the Red Bull Junior Team in 2012 and made his way up the junior categories until 2019, where he got a chance at Toro Rosso alongside Daniil Kvyat. He impressed and was promoted to Red Bull, replacing Pierre Gasly midway through that season. He scored his first podium at the Tuscan GP in 2020

– but partnering Max Verstappen is like the kiss of death, and he was dropped at the end of that season. Williams picked him up for 2022 and the old Albon returned. Alex's family own 12 cats, a dog and 2 horses and he can often be seen on the golf course supporting his girlfriend, Chinese pro Muni 'Lily' He. Never bet on what colour hair Alex will be sporting at the next event – he likes to dye it!

FERNANDO ALONSO

Fernando Alonso is one of the greats of F1. Born on 29 July 1981 in Oviedo, Spain, he began karting at the age of three, using an unwanted gift that his father bought for Alonso's sister. An early test in 1999 for Minardi opened the door for a very young Alonso to sign with the team as a test and development driver. In 2001, aged 19, Alonso became a full-time F1 driver for Minardi, but it was to last only one year as his manager, Flavio Briatore, lined up a move to Benetton (about to become Renault). With no F1 seat, Alonso spent the year honing his craft, completing over 1,600 testing laps.

In 2003, Alonso became a Renault driver, replacing Jenson Button. It took him just two races to become the youngest ever pole-sitter, and in Hungary that year he took his first ever race win – less than a month after his 22nd birthday.

Alonso was magical in an F1 car and was almost faultless on his way to winning his first World Championship in 2005. The following year cemented his place in the history books as he battled with Michael Schumacher (a seven-times champion with 91 race wins under his belt) to become the youngest ever driver to win back-to-back titles.

He switched to McLaren in 2007 alongside F1 debutant Lewis Hamilton. The relationship between them soured quickly, and Alonso fell out with team boss Ron Dennis too. McLaren terminated their contract with Alonso at the end of the season.

Alonso had other chances to win a world title. Driving for Ferrari, he almost took the 2010 and 2012 championships, but Sebastian Vettel beat him both times by the slimmest of margins.

Alonso again moved teams, surprisingly going back to McLaren. It didn't go well … Alonso suffered a mysterious crash in testing and missed the opening race of the season. He was extremely vocal about the Honda engine in the McLaren, complaining it was like a 'GP2 engine'.

A spell away from F1 followed, Alonso racing in the US in the Indy 500 (one of the most iconic motorsport events on the planet) and the World Endurance Championship. We were both at Le Mans in 2018, me reporting on it, Alonso winning it (alongside teammates Sébastien Buemi and

Kazuki Nakajima). It was a glorious 24 hours – Alonso was back. He went on to win Le Mans again in 2019 and became a World Endurance Champion.

After two years out of F1, Alonso was lured back to his old team Renault (now called Alpine) but it didn't work out, so he moved to the new Aston Martin team, owned by Canadian business-magnate Lawrence Stroll. He would drive alongside the owner's son, Lance. It was a puzzling move to many in the paddock; this was the team that Sebastian Vettel had just left, without a win. However, the start of 2023 saw Aston Martin make a massive step up and at the first race for his new team Alonso finished back on the podium – in third place. More good results followed – he secured his 100th F1 podium in Saudi Arabia that year and the bounce was back in his step. He added six more podium finishes to end the season in fourth place in the World Championship.

If you ask around in the paddock, Fernando Alonso is seen as one of the best drivers to have ever graced F1 and someone who should have won more F1 titles. Supremely quick, with an innate feel for whatever car he finds himself in, he is aggressive and unforgiving on track.

DID YOU KNOW? Fernando Alonso is affected by Poland syndrome, which means he is missing his right pectoral muscle.

ALPINE

This is the current team name used by Renault (formerly known as Lotus and Benetton).

Renault are one of the world's largest automotive companies. They first entered F1 in 1977, and have competed in their own right and as an engine supplier to other teams. They won the drivers' and constructors' world titles in 2005 and 2006 with Fernando Alonso as their star driver.

During their time as engine manufacturer, they have won 12 Constructors' Championships and 11 drivers' titles – most notably through their partnership with Red Bull Racing, when they won with Sebastian Vettel at the helm from 2010 to 2013.

APEX

This is one of the first things you will be taught about when learning how to drive a car competitively. You'll hear commentators and drivers talk about the apex a lot.

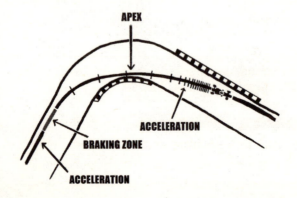

In basic terms, it's the mid-point of a turn; the point where the driver comes closest to the inside of the track. If you 'nail the apex', you optimise the angle of the corner, allowing you to get the most speed out of the car. Speed is good.

ASTON MARTIN

The team in green. Aston Martin first tried their hand at F1 in 1959, but it was short-lived, only lasting just over a year, and they withdrew after the 1960 British Grand Prix without scoring a single point. It took until 2021 for the team to make its return. Canadian business mogul Lawrence Stroll bought a stake in the British car maker, then took over the F1 entry that had been first Jordan, then Spyker and, latterly, Force India and Racing Point. Still following?! He has ploughed money into the team's facilities, building a new factory and wind-tunnel at their Silverstone base, and brought in Fernando Alonso to race alongside Stroll's son, Lance.

AUSTRALIA

Australia hosted its first FIA Formula One World Championship Grand Prix in 1985. The city of Adelaide was chosen as the venue for the season finale and hosted the race, often the title decider, until 1995.

In 1996 the Australian Grand Prix moved to its current home, Albert Park in Melbourne, and, rather than being the last race of the season, it hosted the 1996 season opener. It took just three corners for Albert Park to be the talk of the

How to Read F1

town. On the first lap, Martin Brundle's Jordan was launched into the air after contact with another car. The crash, and Brundle's now famous rush back to the pits to take the spare car for the restart, ensured the first race in Melbourne was a hit.

There have been 15 F1 drivers from Australia since 1950 (when the F1 Championship officially began). Jack Brabham won the World Championship three times, in 1959, 1960 and 1966, and Alan Jones won the title in 1980. More recently Mark Webber, Daniel Ricciardo and Oscar Piastri have all represented their nation.

DID YOU KNOW? An Australian has *never* won the Australian Grand Prix.

B is for

OLIVER BEARMAN, VALTTERI BOTTAS, BRAKING, ROSS BRAWN, BROADCASTING and **JENSON BUTTON**

OLIVER BEARMAN

Bearman was born in Chelmsford, UK, on 8 May 2005, the day Kimi Räikkönen won the Spanish Grand Prix, and the year Fernando Alonso won his first world title. He raced karts and then single-seaters, getting signed for the Ferrari Driver Academy (FDA) at the age of 15, moving to Italy and competing in the junior categories. Appointed reserve and test driver for Ferrari in 2023, he also impressed in his first practice sessions for the Haas team that same year.

Bearman made his F1 debut in 2024, taking the place of Carlos Sainz in the Ferrari in Saudi Arabia after the Spaniard had to have surgery for appendicitis. He had two hours' notice before jumping into the car for the final practice session before qualifying. It was a terrific debut with Bearman finishing seventh, in the points. At just 18, Bearman became the youngest Ferrari debutant ever. He clearly impressed and has been named as a full-time F1 driver for the Haas team from 2025.

VALTTERI BOTTAS

The man of many memes and GIFs, Bottas is almost as famous for getting his bottom out as for his driving skills! First it was #BOTTAS, and now it's Bott-ass.

Bottas came through the ranks of motor racing, taking the GP3 (now F3) title in 2011, the year after he joined Williams as a test driver. In 2013 Bottas had his first race in F1 for

Williams and remained with the team until the end of 2016. At the beginning of 2017, Bottas received a call from Mercedes boss (and his former manager) Toto Wolff offering him the seat left by Nico Rosberg, after the new champion announced his shock retirement from the sport. His time with the team led to 10 race wins, 20 pole positions and an attempt to challenge teammate Lewis Hamilton for the world title. It wasn't to be, and Bottas left Mercedes at the end of 2021, finding a home with Alfa Romeo.

 DID YOU KNOW? It's Lance Corporal Bottas; Valtteri spent a brief time serving in the Finnish army before finding his place in F1.

BRAKING

Braking is essential for going fast. 'What?!' I hear you say. That's right – if you don't get the braking right, it will impact the entire way you drive the corner. It will compromise your ability to hit the apex, take a good line, carry optimal speed through the corner and, of course, get as much power on exit to get the car back up to speed.

Unlike your average road car, an F1 driver has to really stamp on the brake pedal – almost having to stand up in the car. This is why drivers' legs are so strong! A driver's 'feel' is important when it comes to braking; at the start of a race weekend they will brake earlier and use the practice sessions to find their limit.

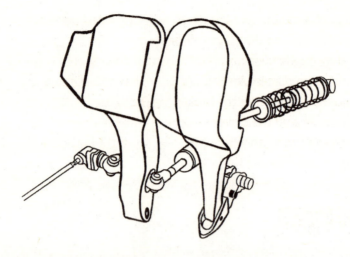

Lewis Hamilton is often referred to as the 'last of the late brakers', a term coined by us media luvvies – but it's true. He often out-brakes his rivals into a corner and makes an overtake stick, something his dad first taught him back in his karting days. Anthony Hamilton would look at the drivers leading the championship to see where they were braking – then he'd go and tell Lewis to brake a couple of metres later, often standing at the point by the track where Lewis should brake. It's a technique that has to be honed over years of practice and can help win races.

Brakes can also be a limiting factor in other ways. They are complex systems, especially the rear brakes, which have a whole set of electronics involved in their application – so, as with anything electrical, these can go wrong. If you're listening to team radio and hear someone say they have a BBW failure, it means a brake-by-wire issue. This can mean the car can't brake any more, and we can all imagine what can happen when a car is going at 320kph without brakes!

Brakes need cooling too. They typically run at temperatures between 700°C and 900°C but if they run too hot for too long, they might seize and fail. They also don't like to run too cold, so in places like Baku or Shanghai, where there are long straights that cool the brakes, by the time the car gets to the corner and the driver stamps on the brake pedal, the brakes are too cool to work optimally, risking a lock-up as the tyres stop rotating.

ROSS BRAWN

One of the lynchpins of modern-day F1, Ross Brawn's name is synonymous with the sport. For me, he has always been one of the key personnel, whether with his own team, Brawn, or with Ferrari, Mercedes or F1 itself.

He was the technical director for championship winners Benetton and Ferrari and was instrumental in helping Michael Schumacher win his seven world titles. After Ferrari, he became team principal of Honda in 2008. When Honda decided to leave the sport at the end of the season Brawn acquired the team, and at the beginning of 2009 Brawn GP arrived at testing with an absolute rocket of an F1 car! Jenson Button dominated the season and won the world title, Brawn GP winning the constructors' title. It was a season, and an achievement, that would be well documented, with Keanu Reeves making a whole TV show about the subject in 2023.

At the same time, Mercedes were keen to return to the sport and bought into Brawn GP at the end of 2009. In 2011,

Brawn and co-owner Nick Fry sold the rest of their shares to Mercedes, who would be reunited with Michael Schumacher for his final years in F1. Brawn carried on as team principal at Mercedes until the end of 2013, when Paddy Lowe and Toto Wolff took over.

Brawn announced his retirement from F1 on 1 February 2014, and told me he was going to spend a lot more time fishing. In 2017, he returned to F1 in a brand-new role: managing director, where he stayed for another five years before deciding the call of his fishing rod was far too great to resist. He retired again at the end of 2022.

Brawn is one of the best technical minds to have graced F1. He played an essential role in winning eight Constructors' Championships and eight Drivers' Championships in total and influenced a generation of technical geniuses.

BROADCASTING

Bernie Ecclestone has been the key figure in negotiating the broadcast rights for Formula One, generating vast amounts of money for both himself and the F1 teams. In the UK, the first race to be shown live on TV was the 1953 British Grand Prix, broadcast on the BBC. From 1979, the BBC signed a deal with Ecclestone for exclusive live broadcast rights, with Murray Walker commentating, to be joined by F1 legend James Hunt. The programme grew in popularity with Steve Rider fronting the show.

ITV bought the rights in 1997 in a deal worth £60m and Murray Walker switched channels and began commentating alongside Martin Brundle. The rights swung back to the BBC at the start of 2009, but it wasn't to last long; a deal was done with Sky Sports for the start of the 2012 season. Sky is now the home of F1 in the UK and in many other territories around the globe. The price to broadcast F1 for Sky: an estimated £200m per season!

I became part of the BBC's F1 team in 2011, joining Radio 5 Live for the Canadian GP. That race is still the longest in F1 history, lasting over four hours, but it was a great introduction to live broadcasting and the art of filling! I have covered every season for BBC Radio since then (over 200 races), hosting the Chequered Flag podcast and bringing the racing alive from the paddock, pit lane and grid.

> **DID YOU KNOW?** Wherever you are in the world, the live coverage of the race – 'the world feed' – is exactly the same. F1 have a broadcasting 'hub' that provides all the trackside cameras for the race. F1's producers and directors make the decisions about what you see, no matter if you are watching in Alabama, USA, or Adelaide, Australia. So next time you get annoyed with the race angle or cut on Sky, or ESPN, or Channel 10, remember, if it happens in the race, it's F1 in control.

JENSON BUTTON

Jenson Alexander Lyons Button was born in Somerset, UK, in 1980. Following in the footsteps of his father John, a former rallycross driver, Button had a passion for motorsport and started karting at the age of eight. His first

How to Read F1

F1 drive was with Williams in 2000, but it took him until 2006 to win his first race, in a Honda at the Hungarian Grand Prix (his 113th race).

At the end of 2008, it seemed like his dreams were about to be shattered. Honda pulled out of F1, and Button found himself without a drive for 2009, until Ross Brawn came to the rescue and signed him to his new team, Brawn GP. Button won the Drivers' Championship and sealed his place in F1 history.

Watching Button was always a masterclass, with his silky-smooth driving style and wet-weather prowess. He won 15 grands prix and stole the hearts of many fans across the world. He drove alongside Lewis Hamilton for a time at McLaren but at the end of 2017 he retired from F1. Button continues to drive in other motorsport disciplines, is now a father himself, and is a pundit for Sky.

One of my favourite memories in F1 is from my first race, the 2011 Canadian Grand Prix, where it rained and rained, and I looked like a drowned rat with a microphone searching the paddock for anyone to talk to. I took refuge from the downpour in an awning outside McLaren, where I found myself a cup of tea, served by none other than Jenson's dad, John. As we huddled in that tent, we shared stories and kept each other topped up with tea. Little did he know that his son, who was placed last in the race after lap 13, would go on to win it.

Jenson Button

DID YOU KNOW? When John Button passed away, Jenson gave out miniature button pins of his dad's infamous pink shirt, so we could all pay tribute to a man who was the life and soul of the F1 paddock. In the 18 years that Button competed in F1, I believe John only missed two of his son's races.

C is for

CALENDAR, CFD, CHAMPAGNE, CHASSIS, COCKPIT, CONSTRUCTORS' CHAMPIONSHIP, CONTRACTS, DAVID COULTHARD, CRASHES and CROWD

CALENDAR

When I first started in F1 in 2011, a calendar for the following year's F1 races was released in the summer break. This used to feature between 16 and 18 races. Now, with F1 expanding and trying to capitalise on the growing markets, the sky is the limit ... or is it? The agreement signed by all the teams, F1 and the FIA states that there can't be more than 25 races in a season. So, currently there is a limit to the number of GPs F1 can run each year. Every year since Covid, more venues are showing interest in hosting a Grand Prix – with the only continent not represented being Africa. The days of 16–18 races a year are long gone – the 2024 calendar featured 24 grands prix. The debate rages on: is it the more the merrier, or have we reached saturation?

CFD

Computational fluid dynamics is a tool used by F1 teams to help design a car which is aerodynamically efficient. An advanced computer program simulates and predicts airflow around the car using complex maths. CFD is now limited depending on how successful a team was the previous year, to allow for greater margins of development as you move down the F1 field. It is used alongside traditional wind-tunnel testing to see how a car (or part of it) will work in motion.

CHAMPAGNE

The tradition of winning a Grand Prix and receiving Champagne dates back many years. In 1950, at the French Grand Prix held among the vineyards of Reims-Gueux, the legendary Argentinian driver Fangio won the race and was presented with a bottle of bubbly from Moët & Chandon. However, the iconic spray didn't arrive until 1967 (the year after Swiss driver Jo Siffert accidently popped his cork at Le Mans, unwittingly spraying the crowd with Champagne). American racer Dan Gurney, after emerging victorious in the Ford in an epic duel with Ferrari, celebrated by popping the Champagne cork and spraying the crowd, including his teammate, his team manager, the photographers and even Henry Ford II and his wife. Gurney has since been credited with instigating one of the most iconic motorsport traditions of all time. It's worth noting that the smell of Champagne and sweat is a pungent aroma that I wouldn't recommend sniffing!

How to Read F1

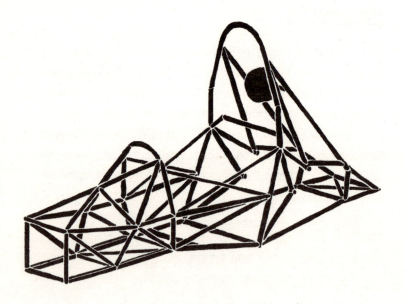

CHASSIS

This is the main part of the race car, which all other parts are built onto. Usually, teams build three chassis to last a year. Drivers usually use one chassis for a whole season, unless they crash their car to the point that they need a new one. A driver can also sometimes believe there is an issue with the chassis and want to change it. Sometimes, a chassis is replaced for 'the spare' when a driver has an impact and the team think it will be quicker to build a new car using a spare chassis and send the damaged chassis back to base for a longer and more detailed investigation. Teams use sophisticated technology to check for damage.

COCKPIT

Like a pilot in a plane, this is the part of the car where the driver sits – it's part of the chassis where the engine and suspension are attached. Unlike in a plane, the driver doesn't sit upright; their legs stretch out in front of them, their bottom slightly lower than anything else, the tops of their feet in line with their knees and shoulders at an angle of about 30 degrees. It's quite an unnatural position.

CONSTRUCTORS' CHAMPIONSHIP

When it comes to the teams, this is the prize they all want. The constructors' title is won by the team that scores the most points in a season, regardless of who is driving the cars. Teams add together the points both their drivers score across a weekend and that gives their Constructors' Championship standings. Prize money is awarded at the end of each season depending on where a team finishes in the standings.

CONTRACTS

With so much money coming into F1 these days, contracts are a big thing. A driver's contract will last for a fixed number of years – maybe just one, but in recent years it has become much more common to have a long-term contract tying a driver to a team for multiple years. The term 'option' is also used, which means either the team or the driver has an option to extend their contract. Often you will hear a driver has signed a '2+1' contract, meaning a contract that lasts two years, with an option to continue for a third year if both parties agree.

As you've probably guessed already, the world of contracts is a very secretive one. Getting hard facts about someone's contract is almost impossible. Sebastian Vettel used to negotiate his own deals with the advice of Bernie Ecclestone, while they played backgammon in his motorhome. Million-pound deals are done, with drivers now having a management team around them taking care of the details. Lewis Hamilton and Max Verstappen are the highest-paid drivers in F1, reportedly earning over £40m annually.

Often referred to as the 'driver merry-go-round', with only 20 seats available there are always going to be drivers that win and lose when a seat becomes free. Imagine it as a giant game of musical chairs, or a set of toppling dominoes. When one driver makes a move, it sets off a chain reaction among the other drivers, and you don't want to be the last driver standing for fear of losing out altogether.

If we look at Lewis Hamilton signing with Ferrari for the 2025 season, it was a move no one expected. It set off a chain of events, firstly with Carlos Sainz losing his seat at Ferrari, when he thought he was about to sign a new contract. Both had to continue to drive the 2024 season in teams that everyone knew they would be leaving at the end of the year – awkward! In total, 13 drivers had their contracts up for renewal at the end of 2024; that's 70 per cent of the drivers. With a Mercedes seat up for grabs, arguably one of the best opportunities on the grid, every driver without a contract for 2025 (and maybe some with a contract) would have been on the phone to Toto Wolff, the boss of Mercedes, to offer their services. Drivers will want to progress from the junior classes too, so there will always be winners and losers; you just need to make sure you have a seat when the music (contract negotiations) stops.

DAVID COULTHARD

This charismatic Scottish driver impressed in his junior career and was appointed as Williams's test driver at the beginning of 1993. The following year, after the death of Ayrton Senna at Imola, Coulthard was asked to take the vacant seat. In the early F1 decades it was quite common to gain your chance after a driver lost their life, but it was far rarer in the 1990s.

Coulthard's first race was the Spanish Grand Prix, just two races after the death of Senna, his hero. His first win came at the 1995 Portuguese Grand Prix. He went on to drive for McLaren and Red Bull, winning 13 races and amassing 62 podiums, before his retirement at the end of 2008. Coulthard is now a mainstay of the F1 paddock, broadcasting and hosting events, and is one of the figureheads behind 'More than Equal', seeking to help find the first female F1 World Champion.

CRASHES

Let's face it, many of us were first drawn to watch F1 and motorsport because of the crashes. In the first three decades of the sport, crashes meant death, as often as not. Safety standards were far less developed than they are today. In the 1950s 15 drivers died in crashes, in the 1960s it was 14, and in the 1970s 12 drivers lost their lives. Sir Jackie Stewart campaigned hard as he watched many friends die behind the wheel. Thanks to him and the developments made in F1 safety, only four drivers died in the 1980s, two in the 1990s and one so far this century.

There have been many infamous crashes and each fan connects with them in very different ways. Think back to footage of Alberto Ascari plunging off the Monaco track and into the Mediterranean Sea in 1955, or of Niki Lauda's car on fire at the Nürburgring in 1976, or the fatal crashes of Ronnie Peterson in 1978 and Gilles Villeneuve in 1982 – sadly, the list goes on.

There are three crashes which will always stick in my mind.

Ayrton Senna – San Marino Grand Prix, 1994

This was the first major crash I watched live on TV. I remember being on the phone to a friend (who was also watching the race) and chatting about strategy and reflecting on the events of the weekend so far (Roland Ratzenberger had crashed and died in qualifying the day before) when suddenly Senna's Williams veered off the circuit, crashing into a concrete wall, killing the Brazilian.

It was a desperately sad time for the sport. I've spoken to countless journalists and F1 personnel who were at the track that weekend, and their recollections are harrowing. It was one of the darkest weekends in the sport's history.

Jules Bianchi – Japanese Grand Prix, 2014

Jules was going to be a star. Already touted as a future Ferrari driver, he had dimples and manners that belied his aggression and determination in a car. It was a pig of a day as the rain fell in Suzuka. The yellow flags came out as a recovery truck moved a stricken car away from the track. Bianchi lost control of his Marussia and crashed heavily into the truck. At the time I was in the paddock reporting for BBC Radio 5 Live and I noticed some of the senior Marussia team members rushing from their garage towards the top of the paddock. It was one of those moments that you just instinctively know something is wrong. The race was won by Lewis Hamilton, but the crowd and paddock were hushed and there were no celebrations. Bianchi was rushed to the local hospital, having suffered severe head injuries. That night was one of my worst in Formula One. I still have a photo of the two of us playing badminton at an event. Honestly, he was so talented and such a beautiful person. He was pronounced dead ten months after the crash, on 17 July 2015. He was just 25 years old.

Romain Grosjean – Bahrain Grand Prix, 2020

Covid kept me away from this race, but I reported on it from home and couldn't believe my eyes when Grosjean's car speared off the track and into a barrier in a ball of fire.

At first, we weren't sure what had happened, so rare are fires like that in Formula One. Luckily, the doctor and safety car were on the scene quickly, and Grosjean was able to somehow pull himself out of the car and away from the burning wreck of his Haas. You couldn't believe what you were seeing. The race was red-flagged, and I remember watching the other drivers standing in the pit lane watching the events unfold, in a state of shock. Grosjean suffered serious burns to his hands but, thanks to his quick thinking, the medics, and the advances in F1 safety, he is now back driving in America.

 DID YOU KNOW? German racing driver Bernd Mayländer has been the safety-car driver since 2000 and is trusted by all the current F1 drivers to guide them safely and slowly (up to 257kph) around the track.

CROWD

Crowds have always been an integral part of F1 racing. In the early days, you used to be able to stand wherever you liked around the track, but fairly quickly it became clear that standing on the inside of a track, while cars roared round just centimetres away from you, was slightly foolhardy. Now, we have grandstands to sit and watch a race, plus general viewing areas – where you can walk around the track and peer in through the safety fences – and a growing number of hospitality suites. Safety is the number-one concern of organisers when it comes to the crowd. There have been some awful accidents in F1's history involving crowd members. Now, fans pack into grandstands adorned in the latest merch, waving flags and banners, and feeling the unique rumble of an F1 start.

DID YOU KNOW? 520,000 fans attended the 1995 Australian Grand Prix in Adelaide across the race weekend. It remains the only race to date to have broken the half-million barrier.

D is for
DEGRADATION, DELTA, DIFFUSER, STEFANO DOMENICALI, DONUTS, DOWNFORCE, DRIVE TO SURVIVE and DRS

DEGRADATION

This term is used to talk about the process in which a tyre loses performance or grip, normally due to the effects of the temperature of the tyre either overheating or underheating, known as 'thermal deg'. It is not to be confused with the way the tyre is worn away – this is called tyre wear and is different.

DELTA

The delta is a time difference between two things, whether that be different cars or lap times. For example, if a car sets a lap time using old, hard tyres, then returns to the track and sets a faster time on new, softer tyres, the difference between those two times is 'the delta'.

DIFFUSER

This is something that is totally relatable to a modern-day car. In fact, you probably have a diffuser on the rear of your car that you can go and have a look at right now! It's right at the back of the car near the floor, where the air flowing under the car exits. The faster the air exits, the lower the air pressure is beneath the car, leading to greater downforce (so more speed). This is a key area of development, and you can see teams looking at other cars up and down the grid to see if they have brought anything new to the diffuser that they may want to add to their own car.

STEFANO DOMENICALI

The president and CEO of Formula One from January 2021, Domenicali is no stranger to cars, having formerly been the chairman and CEO of Lamborghini. Prior to that, he was heavily involved with Ferrari, working his way up to team principal in 2008 and overseeing their Constructors' Championship victory that year, their last win to date.

> DID YOU KNOW? Domenicali used to help out at his local racetrack, which just happened to be the Autodromo Internazionale Enzo e Dino Ferrari, also known as the Imola Circuit. As a child, he would spend weekends in the paddock and the media centre, becoming an avid motorsport enthusiast.

DONUTS

Not the things you eat, but circular tyre burnouts made by winning drivers (if they don't mind being fined!). The best donuts I've seen in Formula One were done by Sebastian Vettel in India in 2013, after he won the race and wrapped up his fourth title with Red Bull. It was to be the last time

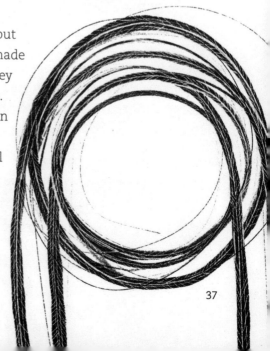

we raced in India and the last time Vettel would win a title. After his donuts, set against the backdrop of the crowd cheering, the tyre smoke began to lift and you could just make out the shape of Vettel, kneeling down, almost in prayer to the car that had brought him so much success. It was a photographer's dream, as are most donuts (both the sugary ones and the rubber ones!).

DOWNFORCE

Measured in 'points', downforce is the aerodynamic force that is applied in a downwards direction as the car travels forwards. The better the downforce, the more the car will 'stick' to the track and improve the way the car can handle the corners.

DRIVE TO SURVIVE

I don't think it's an exaggeration to say this F1 documentary series has changed the whole genre and sport. Before *DTS* came knocking at F1's door, viewer numbers were falling, and as media we kept asking the question: 'Is Formula One dying?' The audience were getting older, and the fan-base was not expanding.

However, when Liberty Media took over F1, Sean Bratches was made managing director of commercial operations. He was a media man and understood the need to generate more publicity and grow the audience. He had the idea to make a documentary series, opening up the paddock to the cameras.

A deal was done between F1 and Netflix, who then brought Box to Box Films on board. The founders, James Gay-Rees and Paul Martin, flew to Brazil and Abu Dhabi in 2017 to speak to Bratches and meet all the team principals. Although they knew hardly anyone in F1 at the time, Gay-Rees had worked on the *Senna* movie and both had made the highly acclaimed Cristiano Ronaldo documentary, *Ronaldo*. Box to Box Films embedded themselves with the teams to film season one, despite Mercedes and Ferrari refusing to take part in the show.

It meant the team had to look for other stories and forced other stars to be found – cue the rise of Guenther Steiner, the Haas team principal. He was a huge success, swearing at everyone and bringing the team's troubled story to life. Who needs Ferrari and Mercedes when you have Haas!

The show lifted the lid on the sport and brought drama and personality to the table. Suddenly, viewers could relate to F1 drivers, and you didn't have to care about the sport to find the series entertaining. Daniel Ricciardo was instantly a fan favourite as he and his parents gave an insight into what life was really like for them. The Netflix series was a success and, unsurprisingly, Mercedes and Ferrari jumped on board for season two. Since then, the cameras have managed to capture some of the key moments in F1's history, unfiltered, unedited and unpredictable.

I was asked to be involved from season three onwards. It was a huge honour to be one of the talking heads on the show, giving a different point-of-view to those representing teams and drivers.

Then came 2021, a year that was decisive, thrilling, and as controversial as they come. Max Verstappen and Lewis Hamilton took the championship all the way to the end of the season. A controversial restart procedure after a safety car in the final race of the season saw Verstappen take the title and Hamilton fail to win his eight World Championship. The Verstappen era had begun. Everyone had an opinion on the events of that season, of that race in Abu Dhabi, and everyone, F1 fan or not, tuned in to watch what happened behind the scenes in that season's *Drive to Survive*.

Some say that race, that championship, was the moment F1 changed from a sport to entertainment. All I know is that F1 has never been more popular. A whole new demographic has been introduced to the sport, and grandstands are now changing, with a more diverse fan-base trying out F1. It's created a very healthy future for the sport, but equally, it has divided opinion (as all good things should), creating a 'new fan' vs 'traditional fan' dynamic. I honestly believe anyone can appreciate the sport in whatever manner they want … as long as I don't have to ask the question, 'Is Formula One dying?' I'm happy!

DRS

The dreaded drag reduction system (DRS), or adjustable rear wing, is an electronic system designed to let a driver adjust the rear wing between two predetermined positions. In essence, it opens a flap in the rear wing, a bit like a letterbox, that allows less drag, hence more efficient aero,

Drive to Survive – DRS

meaning more speed. It can only be used after the first lap of the race is complete, in dry-weather running and, crucially, when a driver is within one second of the car in front. It's a bit like having a magic overtake button, which in effect artificially raises the chance of overtaking. Critics say it makes overtaking in F1 too easy and takes away the skill needed to make a pass without DRS.

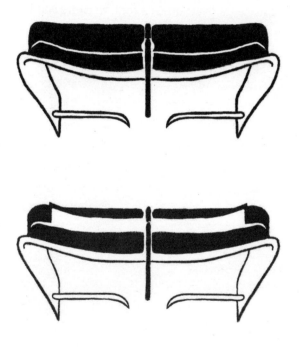

41

E is for
BERNIE ECCLESTONE, ENGINEERS and ENGINES

BERNIE ECCLESTONE

The 'F1 Supremo' – Bernie Ecclestone – is a self-made billionaire responsible for setting up modern-day F1 as we know it. Starting from humble beginnings, Ecclestone first dabbled with bikes selling spare parts and formed a dealership in the 1940s. He started racing and drove in Formula 3 races in 1949, but not with any great success. Ecclestone started managing drivers until he felt the time was right to buy a team in 1971 – Brabham. The team won two world titles in the 1980s and Ecclestone was making an enormous amount of money from the deal. He was rumoured to have invested $120,000 into Brabham and sold the business for over $5m in 1988. All the time he was making valuable connections throughout the paddock, which led to him become chief executive of FOCA (Formula One Constructors Association) in 1974, at the same time as being a team owner. In securing this and subsequent positions, Ecclestone became the main player to negotiate the TV rights for Formula One – splitting the pot between the F1 teams, the FIA and Ecclestone himself, under the company he named FOPA (Formula One Promotions and Administration). It was a move that would lead to Ecclestone effectively 'ruling' F1 for decades, until he ultimately sold to Liberty Media in 2016.

In 1978, Ecclestone hired Sid Watkins to be the official F1 medical doctor, a move to try and improve safety in the sport. Watkins and his work, together with the FIA, made the sport far safer. As soon as Watkins made his recommendations to Ecclestone, he implemented all the changes that were called for, and continued to try and improve safety for all the teams and drivers throughout his time at the helm of F1.

Ecclestone is wily and shrewd and always one beat ahead of you. Interviewing him often felt like you were a fly caught in his web, and it was only a matter of time before you were toast, but he was fascinating. Working in F1 under his helm, you were in no doubt that he ran the roost. Getting a phone call from Ecclestone's office as a rookie journalist in the F1 paddock was something you dreaded. For all of Bernie's money-making schemes and questionable quotes, he was also a very generous man who made the F1 travelling circus what it is today. I remember being sick on the way to Singapore, collapsing on the plane journey. I was taken to hospital and had a number of tests and checks done (I was fine in the end) but when it was time to be discharged, I walked to the payment window and found that the whole bill had been taken care of by Formula One Management – Bernie's business. I had no idea that he felt himself responsible for all of us on the road, but it wasn't the first time, or the last, that he stepped up in times of need. I remember one paddock member receiving a phone call to say their wife was seriously ill – Bernie arranged for his private plane to take the man straight home.

Bernie will always be the 'F1 Supremo' in our heads. He has left a fantastic sport as his legacy. One that was a little bit niche when he first took over but is now a multibillion-dollar global business. Obviously, he has courted controversy along the way – from the rumours linking him to the Great Train Robbery to his association with the Russian leader Vladimir Putin, and his fraud conviction – but without him F1 wouldn't be the sport it is today.

ENGINEERS

When I first started out in F1, a good friend of mine told me the key difference between engineers and mechanics (which is not necessarily obvious): 'A mechanic touches the car; an engineer just watches it.'

This might be an oversimplified statement, but it's not far wrong.

Engineers make up the vast body of the F1 paddock and are the brains of the gang, dreaming up new ways of doing things. There are engineers for almost everything these days, from performance engineers to systems engineers, strategy engineers to tyre engineers.

The literal definition of an engineer is a person who designs, builds or maintains engines, machines or structures. There are so many individual components on an F1 car that need designing, building and maintaining, and that's just on the current cars. Engineers also have to think about the cars for next year, and the cars for the next regulation changes. No wonder the bigger teams have so many personnel and engineers: over a thousand people all feeding into a team. Even the smaller teams have maybe a few hundred, just to run two cars.

DID YOU KNOW? There are some 14,500 individual components on an F1 car and the initial build can cost anywhere between £9 and £15 million.

ENGINES

Engines – or power units, as they are referred to in F1 – used to be a relatively simple subject within F1. They were large, naturally aspirated 4.5-litre engines that were supercharged back in the 1950s. They have been developed heavily over the years to make them more efficient and more road-relevant. There was the V6 turbocharged era from the late 1970s, V8s were introduced at the end of the 1980s at the time of Prost and Senna, then came the V12s. By the end of 1994, Ferrari's Tipo 043 V12 was able to deliver 850 horsepower at 15,800rpm – which is still a record for the most powerful naturally aspirated V12 engine ever used in Formula One. These V12s were ear-splitting, rip-roaring, thunder-clapping behemoths. There was absolutely no chance of falling asleep when one of these was near, let alone over 20 of them starting a Grand Prix. In short, they were LOUD.

Since then, regulations set out by the FIA and F1 have made massive changes to keep the series relevant. In 2014 the sport faced its biggest engine change, shifting from a 2.4-litre V8 engine to a 1.6-litre V6 hybrid engine – the 'hybrid' part allowing for both kinetic and heat-energy-recovery systems, and the fuel flow was limited to 100kg of petrol per hour. It was a massive change which Mercedes mastered best, helping them win eight consecutive F1 titles.

There are currently four engine providers: Mercedes, Renault, Honda and Ferrari. To try and encourage more engine manufacturers to the sport, the next big engine change is coming in 2026. Audi are set to enter and Ford are also returning to F1 (after a gap of almost 20 years) and will supply Red Bull.

Every time we have seen engine changes introduced by the FIA, we've seen a big swing in the power rankings of F1 – the big question ahead of 2026 is who will make the most of the switch in technical regulations and come out on top?

F is for
FATHER/SON, FERRARI, FIA, FLAGS, FLAT-SPOT, FORMATION LAP and the 'F' WORD (F-DUCT)

How to Read F1

FATHER/SON

There's a unique bond between sportsmen and their sons, but F1 takes it to another level. Whether it's a dad giving up everything to pay for his son's karting career or acquiring multimillion-pound companies to support his son's F1 ambitions. However, if you were 'lucky' enough to have an F1 driver as your father, the passion, drive, determination and pressure to follow in their footsteps is almost unavoidable. Whether it's in someone's genes, or is just born out of passion and obsession, there have been many father/son stories throughout F1's history. I've listed some of them below, but let's be under no illusion, there isn't a single driver on the grid in F1 now who didn't rely heavily on their dad (and mum) to make them the driver they are today.

The Hills: Graham and Damon

The first father/son duo to become World Champions. Before his untimely death in 1975, Graham Hill won the Formula One title in 1962 and 1968, and earned the nickname of Mr Monaco, because he won that Grand Prix five times between 1963 and 1969. He also won the Indy 500 and the 24 Hours of Le Mans – 'The Triple Crown' – a feat no one else has ever been able to replicate. Damon Hill won his World Championship in 1996 for Williams and is now a mainstay of F1 broadcasting and a highly respected pundit.

The Rosbergs: Keke and Nico

The second (and so far last) father/son duo to become F1 World Champions. The moustachioed Finn won the championship with Williams in 1982 and his son signed for Williams in 2005, but it wasn't until Nico joined Mercedes, alongside first Michael Schumacher and, later, Lewis Hamilton, that he started to challenge for the title. The 2016 championship was a special one, as Nico and Lewis took the title race right down to the wire. As the lights shone down on the Abu Dhabi track, Nico took second place and sealed the championship. Not long after, he announced his retirement from the sport. He had given it his all. Keke was asked about what it took for his son to win the World Championship. He replied, 'It is remarkable and I admire him for his mental strength and commitment. We have to remember the commitment of somebody like Nico is 110 per cent and it has nothing to do with how I went about being a Formula One driver. I don't think many people from outside, including the media, appreciate the effort that went into this.'

The Villeneuves – Gilles and Jacques

Gilles Villeneuve is one of F1's legends and would surely have won a world title if not for his fatal accident at Zolder in 1982. He was a Ferrari great who was adored by fans and media alike, he was outspoken, and had a natural flair for racing. His son Jacques won the World Championship in 1997 driving a Williams. He is still a fixture of the paddock, getting married to the mother of two of his children, Giulia Marra, at the inaugural Las Vegas Grand Prix in 2023.

The Verstappens – Jos and Max

Jos Verstappen drove for many teams during his ten-year F1 journey, but he was not lucky in his career, with just two podium finishes (still a record for a Dutch driver at the time). Jos loved racing and put all his energy into his son's racing career. Max's mum Sophie was also a great karter. It's no wonder that Max fulfilled his destiny, becoming a multiple World Champion.

The Schumachers – Michael and Mick

Michael Schumacher was one of the greatest drivers of all time, a seven-times World Champion: his legacy will live on forever. Mick graduated to F1 in 2021 with the Haas team, as a Ferrari academy driver, but is now competing in the World Endurance Championship.

FERRARI

'Everybody's a Ferrari fan. Even if they're not, they are a Ferrari fan.' So said Sebastian Vettel in 2016 about the godfather of all Formula One teams, founded by the great Enzo Ferrari. Ferrari had very little formal education, but in 1908 he watched a race at the Circuit de Bologna that would change both his life, and our lives, forever. Watching Felice Nazzaro cross the finish line ignited something in the then ten-year-old Enzo – he wanted to be a racing driver. After serving in the Italian army at the end of World War One, Enzo got a job as a test driver in Milan. He clearly had talent and soon was driving for Alfa Romeo. However, in 1929, at the age of 30, Enzo founded his own company (in close collaboration with Alfa Romeo) called Scuderia Ferrari. It was a gentlemen-drivers club, and had huge success, attracting top drivers like Alberto Ascari and Tazio Nuvolari.

Father/Son – Ferrari

Enzo enjoyed a spell as head of Alfa's racing division, but what he really wanted was his own racing team. With Alfa still owning the rights to the Scuderia Ferrari name, Enzo set up Auto Avio Costruzioni in Maranello, and that is where the magic happened.

In 1945, Enzo got the rights back to his name, and Scuderia Ferrari, as we know it today, was born. The Scuderia first tasted victory in the new F1 World Championship at the British Grand Prix in 1951, as José Froilán González won in his Ferrari 375.

Enzo wasn't really interested in making road cars, he just wanted to make race cars, but the more success he had on track, the more people wanted to buy a Ferrari. In 1953, at a time when the company transitioned between a small number of hand-built cars to series production, the 250 series was launched, the first incarnation of the most beautiful car ever made, the Ferrari 250 GT.

On track, throughout the 1950s and 60s, some of the world's best drivers were drawn to the magic of Ferrari, including Alberto Ascari, Juan Manuel Fangio and John Surtees. Niki Lauda won Ferrari the drivers' world title in 1975 and 1977, then Jody Scheckter (World Champion in 1979) and Gilles

Villeneuve found varying success with the 'Prancing Horse', a name that was garnered from the badge that adorned every Ferrari and is now synonymous with the brand.

After selling half of his business to Fiat in 1969, Enzo Ferrari had a new lease of life. He built the Fiorano test track close to the Maranello factory and launched a whole host of new cars throughout the 1970s and 80s.

In 1988 Enzo Ferrari died, but his legacy lives on. He will always be remembered as one of the greatest names in the automotive world. His passion for racing is the cornerstone of modern-day Formula One.

His replacement was Luca di Montezemolo, who oversaw a golden age for Ferrari. Jean Todt was installed as team principal in 1993, and the Frenchman set about reforming the team. Michael Schumacher, then a two-time World Champion, joined Ferrari for the 1996 season. Todt also brought in key figures like aero man Rory Byrne and technical whizz Ross Brawn to make Ferrari great again. In 1999, they won the Constructors' Championship and Schumacher went on to dominate and win the titles in 2000–4. Ferrari had become the most dominant team in F1 history.

Charles Leclerc is the current star of Ferrari, but in 2025 Lewis Hamilton will fulfil his lifelong dream of driving for the Scuderia as he partners the young Monégasque. Can Ferrari restore their fortunes with Hamilton at the helm? They haven't won a championship since 2008; that's a long time for the Tifosi (the Italian fans) and the sport to wait for the 'Prancing Horse' to get back to winning ways.

FIA

The Federation Internationale de l'Automobile (FIA) was established in 1904 and is the governing body of Formula One (and other motorsports), which means it is responsible for the planning, organisation and governance of the sport. It's had several presidents in its time, including Jean-Marie Balestre, Max Mosley and Jean Todt. Most recently, Mohammed Ben Sulayem was elected as president in 2021.

The FIA is responsible for the rules of F1, which cover the sporting, technical and financial regulations. Every year these regulations get updated and are constantly evolving, along with the sport.

Because 2026 will see such massive changes to the power units, the FIA have already sent out draft regulations to the teams so they can start designing the concepts of these new cars.

FLAGS

There are ten main flags used in motorsport to signal a warning to the drivers, some more obvious than others. The most recognisable are the **chequered flag**, signalling the end of the race or session, and the **red flag**, signalling for drivers to slow and return to the pit lane without overtaking and be prepared to stop if the track is blocked. The other eight are:

Yellow flag – signals danger. A driver must slow sufficiently so they are in full control of the car. No overtaking is

allowed. **Double yellow flags** signal a moderate or serious incident ahead, or that something is blocking the track, so a driver must significantly slow and be prepared to stop.

Green flag – the sign it's all clear after a danger zone. It is also shown at the start of the formation lap (waved at the back of the grid) to show all cars are in place and ready.

Blue flag – a sign that a quicker competitor is close or trying to overtake you. Usually shown to cars that are being lapped.

Black flag – shown along with a driver number, it means a driver has been disqualified from the session and must return to the pit lane immediately.

Black with an orange circle flag – shown when a mechanical issue may be affecting the car and the driver might not be aware of it. The driver must return to the pit lane.

Black and white diagonal flag – shown to make a driver aware that their driving is causing concern and they may be black-flagged if their conduct continues.

White flag – waved in a sector to show there is a service or slow-moving vehicle on track, and held stationary to let drivers know there is a stationary vehicle in the next sector.

Yellow and red striped flag – slippery surface ahead.

FLAT-SPOT

When a driver brakes too heavily or spins, the rubber on the tyre can wear away in one specific spot – the flat-spot. This can lead to severe vibrations, a loss of grip, and may force a driver to pit for replacement tyres.

FORMATION LAP

When all the cars are in their place on the grid for the start of an F1 race, a green flag is waved at the back of the grid and green lights are shown at the front of the grid signalling the start of the formation lap. It's a time for drivers to get one last look at the track and to warm up their tyres ahead of the race. No overtaking is allowed, and it's done at relatively slow speeds. However, there is still jeopardy and drivers have crashed out of the formation lap, their race over before it's even begun. Think back to Brazil 2023 and Charles Leclerc crashing on the formation lap; his hydraulics failed, leaving him unable to steer his Ferrari, and the barriers collected him – race over. A painful moment for any driver.

THE 'F' WORD (F-DUCT)

An ingenious aerodynamic concept, developed by McLaren and quickly copied throughout the Formula One paddock. Originally named project RW80, it was swiftly dubbed the 'F-duct' because the inlet for the system was positioned right beside the letter f of the Vodafone logo.

The idea behind the system was to use air passing over the car to change how the rear wing functioned. This was done by re-routing air from the front of the car and redirecting it to the back, which resulted in decreased drag and increased speed.

However, many thought it was a costly and unfair advantage. The F-duct was banned from 2011. It remains one of the most ingenious but controversial technical developments in the modern era.

G is for

GARAGES, PIERRE GASLY, GOATs, GRID, GRID WALKS, GRAND CHELEM, GRAND PRIX and **GRAVEL**

GARAGES

This is a secure area where the team can set up their equipment and work on their cars. Each garage has a defined space for each car and driver. The garage is usually split down the middle and a driver/car will have their own mechanics and engineers. There is very little of the oil or grease that you might find in your local garage; they are kept immaculately clean and organised, with spillages cleaned up as soon as the car leaves for the track. Garages are now high-tech areas that hold many of the secrets behind a team's successes or failures, so access is strictly controlled. Modern F1 garages have a viewing area for family, friends and guests and are heavily branded. There are up to six garage set-ups that travel around the world in rotation, so there is always one ready for the next race ahead of the team getting there. Usually, it takes a day to turn the blank canvas that is provided by the circuit and the FIA into the branded and fully equipped garage that you see come race day. Garage positions are allotted by the Constructors' Championship standings from the previous year. The first garage, closest to the pit entry lane, normally goes to the title holders, while the last garage is occupied by the tenth-place finishers. There are exceptions to this rule, like Silverstone, but the preference of the 'best' garage usually goes to the team that finished first the previous year.

PIERRE GASLY

Born in Rouen, France, Gasly is the youngest of five children and has four half-brothers. His family has a strong motorsport background; his grandmother was a karting champion in her day. Pierre started karting aged six, where he met fellow racer Anthoine Hubert. The two went to school together and were roommates for several years. Gasly was also friends with Esteban Ocon and Charles Leclerc.

Gasly joined the Red Bull Junior Team in 2014 and won the GP2 series (now Formula 2) in 2016. The following year, he was promoted to the Toro Rosso F1 Team. In 2019, he was again promoted, this time to Red Bull, to drive alongside Max Verstappen. It lasted just 12 races before he was demoted back to Toro Rosso for the Belgium GP. Gasly's long-time friend, Hubert, was tragically killed during the F2 sprint race that weekend. Gasly said after the race, 'I think it was for sure the most emotional pre-race I've ever had. Because you're not ready at 22, 23 years old, to live this kind of moment, to lose one of your best mates.'

Heroically, Gasly came second at that year's Brazilian Grand Prix, and I remember being in tears as he got out of his car and pointed to the sky, remembering his friend. After all he had endured that year, I don't think there was a dry eye to be seen. Gasly got his first F1 win the following year, at the 2020 Italian Grand Prix. In 2023, Gasly joined Alpine, alongside his old karting rival, Ocon.

How to Read F1

GOATs

We could argue until the wee small hours over a drink or two about the definitive list of F1 GOATs – Greatests Of All Time – and maybe we'll get the chance to do that one day. But, for now, this is my top ten based on a mix of their results, skill and personality:

- **Ayrton Senna** – Brazilian three-time World Drivers' Champion (WDC) with McLaren-Honda in 1988, 1990 and 1991. He was just 34 when he died at the 1994 San Marino Grand Prix at Imola. He was one of the most gifted and charismatic drivers F1 has ever seen.

- **Sir Lewis Hamilton** – British seven-time WDC (2008, 2014–15, 2017–20), winning his first title with McLaren and six with Mercedes.

- **Michael Schumacher** – German seven-time WDC (1994–5, 2000–4), winning his first two titles with Benetton before moving to Ferrari and winning a further five.

- **Alain Prost** – French four-time WDC (1985–6, 1989, 1993), winning his first three titles with McLaren and his final title with Williams.

- **Niki Lauda** – Austrian three-time WDC (1975, 1977, 1984), winning two for Ferrari and his final title with McLaren. He went on to innovate and lead many teams, latterly orchestrating the signing of Lewis Hamilton to Mercedes, where Lauda was non-executive chairman.

- » **Max Verstappen** – Dutch three-time WDC (2021–3), all with Red Bull.

- » **Jim Clark** – Scottish two-time WDC in 1963 and 1965. He only ever drove for Lotus. He was killed in a Formula 2 racing accident on 7 April 1968 at Hockenheim, Germany. He was just 32 and had won more Grand Prix races (25) and achieved more pole positions (33) than any other driver at the time. Arguably one of the best 'naturally gifted' drivers we have ever seen.

- » **Sir Jackie Stewart** – Scottish three-time WDC with Tyrrell in 1969, 1971 and 1973.

- » **Fernando Alonso** – Spanish two-time WDC with Renault in 2005 and 2006.

- » **Juan-Manuel Fangio** – Argentine five-time WDC (1951, 1954–7), winning with Alfa Romeo, Mercedes, Ferrari and Maserati. He holds the highest win rate of all time, winning 24 of 52 races (46.15 per cent) and the highest pole average at 29 out of 52 (55.77 per cent).

GRID

The grid refers to the starting positions of the cars in an F1 race. It's determined by the results of qualifying. The car which qualifies with the fastest time starts at the front of the grid on 'pole position'. Each car then takes their spot on the grid, 8m back and on the opposite side of the track to the car in front of them. Cars therefore form two lines in preparation for the start of the race.

How to Read F1

GRID WALKS

One of my favourite parts of a race weekend. The grid is opened one hour before the start of a Grand Prix. This allows each team to send some of their mechanics onto the grid and get everything in place to receive their cars and drivers. This usually consists of high-tech computers, which the car is plugged into, tyres and tyre-warmers, cooling devices, and whatever else the driver or team might need. This is the time I get to go onto the grid, as the F1 cars do their installation laps, trundling through the pits, and finally make their way to the grid.

Most fans, by now, are already in their seats in the grandstands that line the start/finish straight, waving flags, singing songs, and generally enjoying themselves. It makes my job as a pit-lane reporter fun and difficult, as I compete with the crowd and F1 cars to hear myself think. Live radio is a joy, but it also

Grid Walks

takes a lot of energy, planning and skill to be able to do it well. Add in live guests, who may either be a driver or a celebrity, and it's got all the ingredients to go wrong.

There are a bunch of us reporters and presenters who ply their trade walking up and down the grid before a race. Martin Brundle was the first to do a grid walk in 1997. He has described the experience as 'unscripted, unrehearsed car crash television. Whatever happens, happens. And I got to wing it. And I can't throw it back to a studio or have the studio throw it to me. When I happen to find somebody, it flows [...] that puts a lovely sense of urgency into it. I once tried to plan it, and it just didn't work. You've got to take it as it comes.'

It's a dark art, as you are live on TV or radio, describing what you're lucky enough to be seeing, and taking the audience with you on a magical journey. You have several people in your earpiece talking to you, trying to tell you what's happening next, making suggestions of what to ask, telling you where someone is, and all the time counting down to the next segment or the start of the race. Trying to find the person your producer is guiding you towards through your earpiece can be like a game of 'Where's Wally?', and all this time you're trying to avoid being run over by F1 cars getting silently wheeled into place. There is also no order as to who has priority to speak to a celebrity, driver or team principal. My producer always jokes that it's 'elbows out' time as you try and make yourself as wide as possible to hold your position. Then there are the completely unpredictable events, like the time a grid-girl fainted and somehow I ended up holding her board as she was taken from the grid!

How to Read F1

The grid walk happens in
all conditions, and many a
time I've played umbrella
hopscotch, talking
to guests who have
umbrellas and are willing
to share them, keeping
me dry until I've finished
their interview and move
on to my next willing
victim. The grid is the

most live and unplanned part of my weekend; you never
know who you will find, whether they will talk to you or
not, or whether someone else is talking to them at exactly
the time you planned. It's one of the biggest challenges of
an F1 weekend, but also one of the most thrilling things
I've ever done, and when it goes right it's like you've won
the lottery.

It's also a real honour to be able to broadcast the grid walk.
Very few sports let you that close to the action, that close
to the start of an event. Can you imagine a reporter going
onto the pitch at the Superbowl or the World Cup Final and
speaking to the players just after the national anthems
have finished? It just wouldn't happen. Speaking to a driver
just before they take to the start line of a Grand Prix is a
thrilling moment and a real insight into their mindset just
before the lights go out.

GRAND CHELEM

A Grand Chelem (or Grand Slam when translating the French into English) is achieved when an F1 driver scores pole position in qualifying, and then in the race leads every lap, wins the race and records the fastest lap time.

DID YOU KNOW? Only 24 drivers have scored a Grand Chelem in F1 and 61 Grand Chelems have been scored to date.

GRAND PRIX

The literal translation of the French words *Grand Prix* is grand (or big) prize. It was first used in the nineteenth century for horse racing. Motorsport borrowed the phrase in 1906, for the French Grand Prix in Le Mans, and it has now become synonymous with F1.

DID YOU KNOW? To pluralise the phrase, you use 'grands prix'.

GRAVEL

Gravel traps are an important safety feature in F1. They are sections next to the track made up of pebbles and small rocks that drastically slow a car, so if a car has gone off the track, it should prevent it hitting the barriers at high speed and hopefully avoid injury to a driver. As the name suggests, the areas of gravel can also act as a 'trap' for drivers; if you run wide and go into a gravel trap, the car can become beached, leaving you stranded, often bringing out the yellow flags, or even a red flag if the car poses a danger to others.

H is for

HALO, HAAS, LEWIS HAMILTON, HELMETS, CHRISTIAN HORNER, NICO HULKENBERG, JAMES HUNT and HYDRAULICS

HAAS

The only American team on the grid, and the youngest, Haas was the brainchild of Gene Haas, an automotive giant in the States. Haas made their debut in the Australian GP in 2016 with Romain Grosjean and Esteban Gutiérrez. It was a fairy-tale start with Grosjean finishing sixth, earning eight points for the team.

The team was led by Guenther Steiner, who became infamous for his passion (and swearing) while on screen, mainly at his drivers. He generated great publicity for the Haas team, but results on track were harder to come by and the team and Steiner parted ways at the end of 2023.

HALO

This protective barrier, made from strong, lightweight titanium tubing, sits around the driver's head, protecting them from any large object or debris entering the cockpit and causing injury.

It was controversially introduced in 2018, with many drivers complaining it would spoil the 'purity' of the sport or stop the driver from getting out of the car in an emergency. However, the halo has been credited for helping save the lives of Romain Grosjean (Bahrain, 2020), Zhou Guanyu (Silverstone, 2022) and Lewis Hamilton (Monza, 2021), who all had serious crashes that could have ended very differently without it.

HALO

DID YOU KNOW? Since the halo's introduction, the FIA has collected data from 40 crashes, and calculated that the drivers' chances of survival rose by 17 per cent.

LEWIS HAMILTON

Sir Lewis Carl Davidson Hamilton, born in Stevenage, UK, on 7 January 1985 to parents Anthony Hamilton and Carmen Larbalestier, is statistically the most successful F1 driver of all time. I could leave this entry at that, but you probably want to know a little bit more!

He started racing remote-controlled cars when he was just five, finishing second in the national championship, competing against adults. His father bought him a go-kart for Christmas the next year, and there the story began.

Lewis's parents split when he was two and he lived with his mum at first (and two older stepsisters). When he was 12, he moved in with his dad and stepmum Linda, and their son Nicolas. It was tough finding money to fund karting, but Lewis showed a natural ability and the family cobbled together enough money to keep the dream alive.

The question I get asked the most about F1 is, 'What's Lewis Hamilton really like?' Often people think he's arrogant, moody and prone to the odd tantrum; well, I can say that's not my experience of Sir Lewis. He might have the odd 'bad day' when he doesn't want to speak to the media and gives you a less than helpful answer to a question, but don't we all have days like that? Throughout my time in motorsport and F1, Lewis has always been kind, courteous, thoughtful and eloquent.

One of my first big interviews with him was at the Brazilian Grand Prix in 2013, where he spoke candidly about his time growing up: 'Me and my dad spent a lot of time in the back of our van, eating Pot Noodles and working on the go-kart my dad bought me. It wasn't the newest, or the fastest. We went through the old tyres that other competitors had thrown away after one day and used those. We couldn't afford the best, so we had to be smart about the way we went karting.'

It was clear from the passion and determination in Hamilton's voice that those memories are filled with pride and pain. As the only black family on the karting circuit, and not coming from great wealth, the Hamiltons had it tough. Luckily for Lewis, his talent shone through, although

Lewis Hamilton

I suspect that made it worse at times, as he was subjected to discrimination and abuse throughout his time driving.

After two years karting, Hamilton became the youngest driver to win the British cadet karting championship, aged ten, and was invited to the Autosport Awards, a moment that would change his life. He approached Ron Dennis, the then boss of McLaren, and asked him for an autograph. Hamilton introduced himself, saying he had won the British Championship and that one day he wanted to be racing his cars. Dennis then wrote in Hamilton's autograph book, 'Phone me in nine years, we'll sort something out.'

It didn't take nine years. Dennis called Hamilton at the end of 1998 and offered him a role in the McLaren driver development programme, with an option on a future F1 seat. He was 13 years old.

Hamilton won the British Formula Renault title in 2003, and in 2006 he won the GP2 title. It was time for Lewis to become a Formula One driver, where he would partner two-time World Champion Fernando Alonso. Both men came close to winning the championship in 2007, but Hamilton was beaten by Kimi Räikkönen by just one point. Hamilton was repaid with a multimillion-pound contract to stay at McLaren until 2012.

Hamilton won his first F1 title the following year in a thrilling finale in Brazil. 'It's pretty much impossible to put into words, I am still speechless […] It has been such a long journey […] I'm so thrilled to be able to do this for everyone,' Hamilton said after the race.

It would be another six years before he would win another World Championship, and it came after he left McLaren for Mercedes. It was a move engineered by Niki Lauda, who managed to woo Hamilton away from the team he signed for aged 13.

In 2014, with new engine regulations, Mercedes became the dominant team, perfectly interpreting and applying the technology behind the new hybrid-turbo engines. With Lewis racing alongside his former karting teammate Nico Rosberg, Mercedes won 16 of the 19 races, taking the constructors' title and a long-awaited second world title for Hamilton. 'This one definitely feels sweeter than the first,' he said after the race. 'It's been an incredible year and I've been very blessed to have a great team around me.'

Hamilton won again in 2015, but Rosberg came back with renewed energy and took the title in the season finale in 2016, then promptly retired. Hamilton raced alongside Valtteri Bottas in 2017 and won the title in another dominant display. He went on to win in the next three seasons, landing an incredible seven world titles.

2021 was a tough year as Hamilton went up against Max Verstappen at Red Bull. It was a season full of controversy, with the pair crashing at Silverstone and taking each other out at Monza. The atmosphere in the paddock was acidic, with respective team bosses, Toto Wolff and Christian Horner, taking low blows at each other at every opportunity. It was dramatic, spellbinding, and an absolute tonic to us journalists, who had at times in previous years wondered if this was still the sport we had fallen in love with.

Abu Dhabi 2021 was something else ...

Going into the race both Lewis and Max had equal points. Whoever finished in front of the other would win the world title. With Hamilton leading comfortably with only a handful of laps to go, it looked like he was going to win a record-breaking eighth world title. Then a crash involving Nicholas Latifi brought out the safety car and, some would say, changed the course of F1 history. Verstappen now had time to come in for fresh tyres. It was a gamble for Max but gave him one last chance to at least try something. He rejoined the race with five lapped cars between him and Hamilton. After numerous radio calls from Christian Horner, race director Michael Masi allowed just these five cars to overtake the safety car, allowing

How to Read F1

Max to close up to Lewis (FIA rules stated that all lapped cars should be allowed to un-lap themselves, which – if all the cars had unlapped themselves – would have taken longer, past the end of the race, and guaranteed Hamilton's victory).

When the race restarted it meant Lewis, still on old tyres, was now a sitting duck; Max swooped past him to take his first title. As the fireworks exploded above our heads, the whole paddock was shell-shocked – what had just happened? Mercedes protested vehemently and no one knew what was going on. It was an evening like nothing else I've ever experienced in my career. After four hours the protests were rejected, and Max was World Champion.

There was no word from Hamilton, who retreated into the shadows, where he stayed for the whole winter. Would he ever race again? Just before testing in 2022, a relieved Mercedes confirmed Hamilton would return to F1.

However, at the start of 2024, rumours started to swirl; the whisper was Hamilton would join Ferrari. It was a fast-developing story – moving from rumour, to fact, to perfectly timed statements from Mercedes and Ferrari, confirming Hamilton's move to Ferrari for 2025. It was another bold move from Hamilton, ending 12 years with Mercedes.

Lewis is much more than just an F1 champion. He's always been a man driven by his past and knows how valuable his platform is. He founded Mission 44, to address diversity and equality issues within motorsport, and has often said what drives him isn't just winning, it's about making a change. Hamilton has made a stand for human rights and famously wore his rainbow helmet at the first race in Saudi Arabia, a country where homosexuality is illegal.

Hamilton leads a jet-set lifestyle: music and fashion are as essential to him as training and his vegan diet. He was knighted in 2021, taking his mum to the ceremony. The boy from Stevenage who learned karate when he was five to defend himself from bullies is now a global brand, with a multimillion-pound contract taking him into his fourth decade. So, what is Lewis Hamilton like? He's unique: hugely talented, an inspiration and, without him, F1 wouldn't be the sport it is today.

DID YOU KNOW? Lewis is reputed to be worth $320 million and is one of the highest-paid British sportsmen.

HELMETS

In the early days of F1, cloth and leather caps and goggles were used to keep dust out of drivers' eyes. However, in 1954 Bell introduced the first helmet as we know it today. It was later certified by the Snell Memorial Foundation, an organisation that was set up in 1957, following the death of William 'Pete' Snell from a head injury in a motor race.

In 1968, Dan Gurney (the same F1 driver responsible for Champagne celebrations) worked with Bell to design a full-face helmet. Gurney was unusually tall for an F1 driver and was fed up with gravel and debris hitting his face. (Nomex, a fire-retardant lining that reduced the likelihood of burns in a fire, was also introduced around this time.)

The introduction of full-face helmets was not only safer but gave drivers the chance to personalise their helmet designs. I remember Nigel Mansell's Union Jack arrow design, Ronnie Peterson's black striped helmet and, of course, Senna's yellow helmet with green and blue stripes that influenced Hamilton's design from karting to F1.

The HANS (head and neck support) device was introduced in 2003 and is now compulsory in most motorsports. The device is effectively a collar that is worn over the driver's shoulders and connects to the back of their helmet, preventing excessive head and neck movement in an accident.

CHRISTIAN HORNER

You may have heard of the adage, the best football players rarely make the best football managers. Well, Christian Horner worked that out pretty quickly and has gone on to earn his place as 'the Arsène Wenger of F1'.

A former racing driver turned team boss, Horner is one of the leading figures in F1. He was born in Leamington Spa on 16 November 1973 and developed a passion for cars (both his grandfather and dad worked in the automotive world). He started karting and progressed up the junior categories, until he got to Formula 3000, when he realised he was unlikely to achieve his dream of becoming an F1 driver, so wisely turned his attention to running a team.

He set up Arden and went looking for a second-hand trailer: enter a certain Helmut Marko, the boss of the Red Bull Junior Team, who happened to be selling a trailer. It was a chance meeting which led to them working together ever since. Arden won the F3000 Championship in 2003 and when Red Bull co-founder Dietrich Mateschitz bought the Jaguar F1 team at the end of 2004, he asked Marko to enlist Horner to be team principal – the youngest in F1 history at just 32.

Horner signed David Coulthard and Christian Klien as his first drivers and at the end of 2005 he signed Adrian Newey to be the team's chief technical officer. It was a masterstroke.

Sebastian Vettel joined Mark Webber from 2009, and the team finished second in the Constructors' Championship, the pair taking six wins between them. From 2010, Horner steered Red Bull to four consecutive constructors' and drivers' titles. Red Bull and Horner became one of the most successful partnerships in F1 history. Horner's management style was questioned in 2013 when Vettel and Webber seemingly went to war with each other, but he rode it out.

In 2016 Max Verstappen joined Red Bull. He was just 18 at the time, but Horner realised his potential and stole him away from Mercedes, who wanted to sign Max but didn't have a race seat for him.

Horner and Newey formed one of the most formidable pairings in F1 history, a partnership that will end in 2025 when Newey leaves. Red Bull have the fastest car, the fastest driver, and make the fastest pit stops, and are one of the most dominant teams since F1 began.

Former Spice Girl Geri Halliwell and Horner married in 2015 and the two of them feature heavily in *Drive to Survive*, especially at the end of 2022, when Red Bull were found to have broken the new cost-cap rules, Horner repeatedly saying, 'We have done nothing wrong.' It was a pivotal moment in Horner's management and resulted in the team being fined and having sporting sanctions imposed on them.

Controversy has continued to follow Horner, and the Red Bull team were destabilised with accusations against Horner of inappropriate and controlling behaviour towards a female employee at the start of 2024, which he has strongly denied, and which an internal investigation cleared him of. Horner remains at the helm of Red Bull, the team he has led for 20 years.

NICO HULKENBERG

Before graduating to F1 with Williams in 2010, this German driver was the 2009 GP2 champion. Despite his epic pole position for the team in Brazil (their first for five years), he lost his seat at the end of the year. He's had spells with Force India as test/reserve driver, and has driven for Sauber, Renault, Racing Point and Aston Martin, before landing a seat with Haas, alongside Kevin Magnussen.

At the end of 2023, Hulkenberg held the unwanted record of the most F1 race starts without a podium.

JAMES HUNT

This British racing driver won the World Championship in 1976 with McLaren and won the hearts of many a fan as he lived his life to the absolute limit, both on and off the track. He was nicknamed 'Hunt the Shunt' in his early days, he crashed so many cars on his way to Formula One. While he was confident and popular off the track, he was an intense and anxious driver, often struck down with such fear before a race he would be sick on the grid, and he would shake so much that his car would vibrate. He was full of adrenaline and testosterone, and that led to success in races, but also in his conquests away from racing; James was a ladies' man who reportedly slept with over 5,000 women. He had the phrase 'Sex, breakfast of champions' embroidered on his overalls.

James joked that his reputation for road rage made rivals move out of his way, '... because they thought I was barking mad!' The year he won the championship, he was up against his good friend Niki Lauda. It was the year Lauda almost died in a car fire at the Nürburgring. Lauda came back to battle for the title, and it went down to the last race of the season, in Japan. It was pouring with rain and Lauda decided it was too dangerous to drive. Hunt stayed out, driving through the rain to finish third and become World Champion.

He was the 'Golden Boy' of Formula One and after his retirement in 1979 he and Murray Walker become a dynamic duo behind the mic, commentating on F1 races for the BBC.

He died on 15 June 1993, suffering a massive heart attack, aged just 45. The whole motorsport world was deeply saddened that he had died so young. Niki Lauda commented, 'For me, James was the most charismatic personality who's ever been in Formula One.'

HYDRAULICS

Hydraulics: the science of liquid in motion. An essential part of F1 nowadays, hydraulics are used in gear-shifting, the engine, power-steering, the clutch and DRS (drag reduction system) to name just a few. If a team report a hydraulics leak or failure, this can often result in damage to the engine or gearbox, so the car needs to be stopped immediately and often leads to a retirement.

DID YOU KNOW? Hydraulic fluid is dyed red to help teams identify it from other fluids.

I is for INNOVATION

INNOVATION

Have you ever dreamed of driving an F1 car? Well, you're not a million miles away from it every time you get in your road car, because what happens on track, doesn't just stay on track. If it's successful, normally it finds its way into mass production. It's one of the things us F1 geeks love to talk about – *the innovation of F1*. From safety to efficiency, sustainability and driver comfort, all these things have influenced how your car is designed and made today.

> » **Rear-view mirrors:** Developed by Ray Harroun, a driver in the inaugural Indy 500 in 1911, so he could see his rivals. It must have worked well because he went on to win the race that year.

> » **Steering wheels:** Ever wondered why you don't have to fiddle around for the buttons to control your radio? Thank F1 designers. The development of control buttons on your steering wheel can be traced back to F1 steering wheels. From paddle shifts on the back of a steering wheel to setting cruise control, this is all thanks to the buttons on an F1 car.

DID YOU KNOW? An F1 steering wheel costs roughly $60,000 to make, and a driver can get through three or four in a year.

Innovation

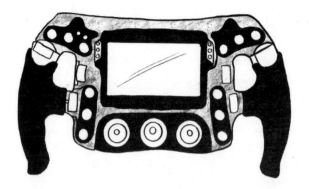

- » **Hybrid powertrains:** Many think it was a dark day for Formula One when the roaring V12 and V10 engines were ruled out, but it has led to some significant developments that are changing the world. In 2014, all F1 cars had to use a hybrid powertrain – meaning the power recovered from the heat of the engine and via the braking energy could be stored in a lithium-ion battery, offering drivers more power as required. This led the way for your car to be more energy-efficient, and now hybrid/battery power can be seen in every car produced.

- » **Carbon fibre:** In 1981, McLaren made the MP4/1 – it was the first race chassis made of carbon fibre and not aluminium, meaning it was stronger, stiffer and lighter. F1 driver John Watson described it as 'like flying in Concorde when you've only ever flown in a 707'. It went on to revolutionise the world of car design.

- » **Active suspension:** One of the most prominent F1 technologies that's now commonplace in mainstream vehicles. It empowers a car to adapt its chassis level in response to road conditions, resulting in improved traction and cornering capabilities.

» **Fuels:** hydrogen, synthetic and biofuels are currently undergoing testing for F1 and other race cars. Given the increasing emphasis on eco-friendly energy sources, this is now the technology battle that F1 is taking on, which could lead to the phasing out of fossil fuel for good.

J is for
JAPAN, JUMP START and JUNIOR CATEGORIES

How to Read F1

JAPAN

The Japanese fans are like no others in the world. They are mad for F1 and pour into the circuit when it's still dark. As the sun rises, they sit in respectful silence until the cars come out on track. They also love to give gifts, even to the likes of me! I was once greeted by a fan at a train station in Yokkaichi, his hands raised in the air, merrily shouting my name, and then presenting me with a gift of biscuits. How he knew I would be there, I have no idea.

The first F1 race in Japan took place in 1976 at the Fuji Speedway. It was the title decider between Hunt and Lauda. As the rain poured down Lauda retired for safety reasons while Hunt finished third to take the title. The following year Hunt won the race but the event was overshadowed by the tragedy that unfolded when Gilles Villeneuve and Ronnie Peterson collided, and two spectators were killed.

It took ten years for racing to return to Japan. Suzuka was the new venue, a circuit built within a funfair and owned by Honda, who use it as a test track. A unique circuit, designed

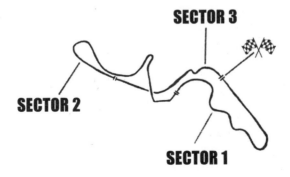

in a figure of eight, it's a track that thrills both drivers and fans. The Japanese Grand Prix has been the title decider 13 times, and Michael Schumacher has won the most times, with six victories.

There have been 21 Japanese drivers who have competed in F1, including Taki Inoue, Takuma Sato, Kamui Kobayashi and current driver Yuki Tsunoda.

JUMP START

When a driver moves off from their grid position before the start of the race has been signalled it's called a jump start. Sensors detect any movement before the start lights are switched off and the FIA will issue a penalty.

JUNIOR CATEGORIES

No one gets to compete in F1 before they've had 'some' success in junior categories. Most people start their driving careers in karting. They then enter single-seater cars, climbing from regional and international Formula 4 cars, through to regional then international Formula 3, and finally Formula 2. This is the feeder series for Formula One, where most of the current F1 drivers have won the championship, or at least performed well in that series.

DID YOU KNOW? The rules of F2 mean a driver can't compete in the championship once they have won the title.

How to Read F1

F1 Academy is the newest feeder series, designed to bring females into the sport. Racing F4 cars, the drivers are affiliated with the F1 teams, building a defined route for young women to get into the higher levels of motorsport.

K is for
KARTING and KERS

KARTING

This is an essential tool to learn how to drive an F1 car and most young drivers find their feet at kart tracks around the world. There are regional, national and international competitions that act as a foundation for future stars. Young drivers will hope to get signed by a Formula One team's development programme (like Lewis Hamilton did).

Karting is a true test of driver skill, unlike Formula One, where the worst cars on the grid can't compete with the best cars no matter how talented the driver is. Yes, some karts are better than others, and drivers with more funding have access to better equipment, but the difference in karting is less profound, allowing the best drivers to rise to the top.

KERS (KINETIC ENERGY RECOVERY SYSTEM)

This is a system designed to recover a moving vehicle's kinetic energy under braking. The rear wheels generate energy, which goes through the drive shaft and into a motor, charging up the battery. The energy is thus 'harvested' and, using a button on the steering wheel, the driver can choose when to deploy it and how much to use, to either attack or defend.

L is for
LAPS, NIKI LAUDA, CHARLES LECLERC, LIGHTS OUT and LELLA LOMBARDI

LAPS

Every F1 race has a set number of laps, a lap being one completed circuit of the track. The number of laps is set out by the rules of F1, with each race being no shorter then 305km. Monaco, at a circuit-length of just 3.337km, has the greatest number of laps with 78, while Spa-Francorchamps is 7km long and needs just 44 laps to constitute a Grand Prix.

NIKI LAUDA

Born in Vienna in February 1949, Lauda was a motor racing icon and successful businessman. He was a three-time World Champion, taking the title for Ferrari in 1975 and 1977, and for McLaren in 1984.

He is probably best known for his battles on track with James Hunt and for surviving a crash at the Nürburgring in 1976. He suffered third-degree burns that left him scarred for life, he inhaled toxic gases that damaged his lungs, and received the last rites in hospital. Yet just 40 days after the crash he returned to race in F1, finishing fourth in the Italian Grand Prix.

After retiring, Lauda went on to become an entrepreneur, setting up his own airline. He later became a non-executive chairman for the Mercedes F1 team, was instrumental in bringing Lewis Hamilton to the team, and helped Mercedes to become the dominant force in 2014–21.

There are no words that can describe how fabulous Niki was. Always seen in the paddock with his red baseball cap, he had a sparkle in his eyes and would tell the most outrageous stories that could never be published. He was a hoot, and it was a real privilege to spend time with him.

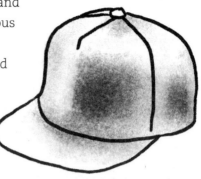

He passed away aged 70, but his spirit (and red cap) will live on in F1 forever. The rear of the Mercedes car has a three-pointed star motif and one of the stars is painted red in his honour. His cap still hangs on the headset mount in the Mercedes garage, a lasting tribute to one of the greatest the sport has ever seen. A statement released by his family after his death read, 'His unique achievements as an athlete and entrepreneur are and will remain unforgettable, his tireless zest for action, his straightforwardness and his courage remain a role model and a benchmark for all of us.'

CHARLES LECLERC

This Monégasque driver, born on 16 October 1997, has competed for Ferrari since 2019. He is the middle child of three boys and followed in the family tradition of racing cars; his father Hervé drove in Formula 3 in the 1980s and 90s.

Leclerc began in karting and won the French Championship in 2005, 2006 and 2008. He was signed up by Nicolas Todt (Jean Todt's son), racing in the junior categories with ART Grand Prix and taking the GP3 title in his debut year. In 2016, he joined the Ferrari Driver Academy.

How to Read F1

I first interviewed Leclerc that year in Spa, and he was charming! With his dimples and scruffy brown hair, he spoke about his hopes of reaching F1. His godfather was the late Jules Bianchi, someone I was lucky enough to spend time with. It was clear that Charles had learned a lot from Jules.

In 2017, Leclerc won the F2 title racing for Prema, in a year that would be full of tremendous highs and devastating lows. He drove his first Ferrari F1 car in a mid-season test in Hungary. However, his father died after a long illness just four days before Leclerc was due to compete in the Azerbaijan F2 race. In one of the most moving scenes I have witnessed, Charles won the feature race and stood on the podium, the paddock gathering underneath to pay tribute to his dad, but also to appreciate what mental strength it must have taken for Charles to even get behind the wheel of his car, let alone win.

He stepped up to F1 to compete with Sauber for the 2018 season before being announced as a Ferrari driver in 2019.

Kind, thoughtful, often berating himself over the team radio if he gets something wrong or crashes, Leclerc is arguably the fastest man over one lap in F1. In 2025 he will go head-to-head with Lewis Hamilton at Ferrari – let's see who is faster then.

DID YOU KNOW? After being challenged by a fan during Covid, Leclerc dressed up as a giant banana and played *Fortnite* and *F1 Live*.

LIGHTS OUT

A phrase synonymous with F1 starts and, although originally used by commentator Ben Edwards, now Sky Sports F1 commentator David Croft begins every F1 race with 'It's lights out and away we go!'

As the start procedure gets under way, the five lights on the gantry above the grid, just in front of the drivers, light up one at a time, until all five lights are shining red. These are held for a random period (so no driver can predict the exact timing) then all five lights go out and the race is under way.

LELLA LOMBARDI

Italian Lombardi is the first and only female driver to have scored points in F1. Actually, she scored half a point at the Spanish Grand Prix in 1975 (half-points were awarded after the race was cut short because of a crash which killed four spectators). She started 12 F1 races between 1974 and 1976, first driving a Brabham in qualifying at the British Grand Prix in 1974. It was a time when there were more drivers in qualifying than places on the grid and Lella, along with nine other drivers, didn't qualify for the Grand Prix.

M is for
KEVIN MAGNUSSEN, MARBLES, MARSHALS, MCLAREN, MECHANICS, MEDIA, MERCEDES, MONACO and MONEY

KEVIN MAGNUSSEN

Danish racing driver born in 1992, the son of four-time Le Mans class winner and former F1 driver Jan Magnussen. Kevin started karting, stepped up to single-seater racing and was signed by McLaren's young driver programme. His first F1 race was Australia 2014, where he finished in second place (third on track but he was promoted when Daniel Ricciardo was disqualified). It was quite some entry to the F1 world.

Magnussen drove for Renault in 2016, before moving to new team Haas in 2017, where he stayed until 2020. In 2021, Magnussen left F1 to focus on sportscar racing, taking part in the 24 Hours of Le Mans with his dad. He was all set to race in the World Endurance Championship in 2022 when, unexpectedly, Haas asked him to return to F1, for whom he has driven ever since.

He is a devoted father of two girls, loves a tattoo and has a laid-back, affable manner outside the car. However, his driving style is aggressive, elbows-out, and has earned him a bad-boy reputation.

MARBLES

As the tyres are used in a race, tiny pieces of rubber wear off them and accumulate on the track off the racing line. Given the name 'marbles', these pieces of rubber are small, round and very slippery (hence the name) and can cause the driver to lock up or even lose control of their car.

MARSHALS

A voluntary role, marshals are essential for racing to take place safely. Marshals are course officials with many responsibilities: observing spectators and making sure they are safe and not interfering with the race; helping remove stranded cars from the track; picking up debris; or sometimes even moving live animals from the track. Marshals control the flags and buttons used to communicate with race control and the drivers during sessions.

MCLAREN

Founded by New Zealander Bruce McLaren in 1963, the team have won 12 Drivers' Championships and 8 constructors' titles.

McLaren's father was a racer and owned a garage, meaning Bruce had access to cars from a young age. He was enthralled, and his passion and talent led him to the UK and to F1, where, after several years with Cooper, he formed his own team.

The McLaren team entered their first Grand Prix in 1966 at Monaco. Their first win came two years later, at the 1968 Belgium Grand Prix, with Bruce McLaren at the wheel of their now synonymous papaya-coloured car. The team also had great success in the Can-Am Championship in North America, but McLaren tragically died in 1970, during a test for his Can-Am car at Goodwood; the team race on in his name with his spirit at their heart.

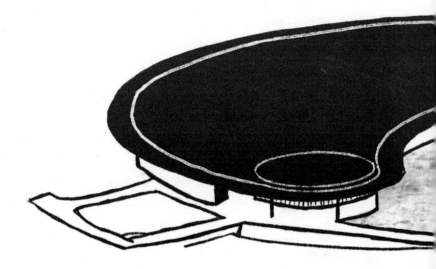

The team won their first Constructors' Championship in 1974, and Emerson Fittipaldi and James Hunt won the drivers' titles racing for McLaren in 1974 and 1976 respectively. In 1981, Sir Ron Dennis took over as team principal, and McLaren entered their most successful era, with Niki Lauda, Alain Prost and Ayrton Senna winning seven Drivers' Championships and six Constructors' Championships between them, making Dennis statistically the greatest team boss in F1 history.

The team is based in Woking, Surrey, at the legendary McLaren Technology Centre (MTC). Ron Dennis employed architect Norman Foster to design the now iconic semicircular, glass-fronted building. If you are ever lucky enough to go to the MTC, prepare yourself for an experience like no other. It has a certain Bond villain vibe as you glide around the long, arched driveway, with a lake reflecting the curved building on your right.

McLaren

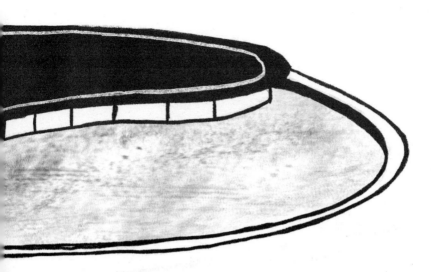

As you enter the MTC you would be excused for thinking you have stepped into a museum, with McLarens from the 1960s to today displayed beautifully in the giant lobby. There isn't an oil-stained workshop in site. Rumour has it that Dennis was so fastidious about the design of the building that even the screws were tightened to an exact vertical angle so they can't collect dust.

American businessman and racer Zak Brown is McLaren's current CEO and team principal, having taken over in 2016, returning the car to its traditional papaya colour.

McLaren have attracted some of the best F1 drivers in history: James Hunt, Niki Lauda, Alain Prost, Ayrton Senna, Mika Häkkinen, David Coulthard and Kimi Räikkönen, with Jenson Button and Lewis Hamilton teaming up in the 2010s. Lando Norris and Oscar Piastri are McLaren's current drivers, both hoping they can return the team to title-winning ways.

How to Read F1

The team last won the Constructors' Championship in 1998, and the drivers' title in 2008 with Hamilton.

DID YOU KNOW? The first female to race for McLaren was New Zealand rally star Emma Gilmour. She wore the famous papaya in the Extreme E Championship in 2022-3.

MECHANICS

These are the people who actually work on the cars. Each team has a chief mechanic overseeing the garage. Then, each car has a number-one mechanic, who is responsible for their car and all the people who work on it. Each car has around seven mechanics, each with their own dedicated role. There will also be a tyre expert and a fuelling expert. Then there is the pit crew, made up of 22 team members from both sides of the garage. This team works in unison to perform the fastest pit stops for both drivers.

MEDIA

Formula One has gained traction in the last few years, which means more people want to know what's going on, and there is a travelling media team who supply newspapers around the world with F1 reports and features. There is also the online community, a rapidly growing number of websites offering their take on events in F1. There are the broadcasters, who usually work from the TV compound, and then there are the radio teams (that's my lot) who broadcast live sessions and reports from the pit lane.

Every paddock contains a media centre, a fascinating place where journalists and broadcasters from around the world congregate to bring you the latest from F1. You must be an accredited journalist to earn a place in the media centre, but there are about a thousand members of the media travelling to F1 races every year.

MERCEDES

Known as the Silver Arrows, Mercedes first competed in F1 in 1954 with instant success, Juan Manuel Fangio winning their debut race and the title. Fangio and Stirling Moss finished first and second the following year, but after a horrific crash at the 1955 24 Hours of Le Mans, in which Mercedes driver Pierre Levegh and over 80 spectators were killed, the team withdrew from all motorsport.

Mercedes didn't return until 1993, when they teamed up with Sauber to supply their engines. The partnership only lasted two years before Mercedes switched to McLaren. Together, they won three drivers' titles and one constructors' title between 1995 and 2009. In 2009, Mercedes supplied engines to Brawn GP, who won both the constructors' and drivers' titles that year.

This led the way for Mercedes to return to F1 as a team. They bought Brawn GP at the end of 2009 and Nico Rosberg and Michael Schumacher were announced as their drivers, but it was a relatively underwhelming return to the sport.

How to Read F1

It wasn't until Toto Wolff moved from Williams to Mercedes that the team returned to winning ways. Together with Niki Lauda as non-executive chairman, they secured Lewis Hamilton to drive for them in 2013, replacing the retiring Schumacher. From 2014 the team won seven consecutive F1 constructors' titles, with Hamilton winning the Drivers' Championship six times and Nico Rosberg winning once.

MONACO

The jewel in F1's crown, this blue-riband event has thrilled drivers, fans and celebrities for over 80 years. Run since 1929, it's one of the three races that make up the Triple Crown, the elusive title given to anyone who wins the Monaco GP, the Indy 500 and 24 Hours of Le Mans. Only one person has ever done this, the legendary Graham Hill.

The idea to race around the tight and twisty streets of Monaco was that of Antony Noghès, under the auspices of Prince Louis II. With hay bales separating drivers from the perilous harbour, and a tunnel and swimming pool to navigate, not to mention the tight hairpin by the hotel on the hill and the small tobacco shop that drivers had to avoid on their way past the ocean, who wouldn't find the race thrilling? The best drivers have always shown their skill in Monaco, with Ayrton Senna, Graham Hill, Michael Schumacher and Alain Prost all having won multiple times.

Qualifying is everything here. The narrow streets of the principality make overtaking almost impossible, so if you

Mercedes – Monaco

don't start on the front row of the grid on Sunday, your chances of winning are very slim. What the race lacks in excitement, however, qualifying makes up for, as the drivers have to be perfect to be the fastest around one lap of the Monte-Carlo course. One centimetre too close to the barriers, a moment of lost concentration, the slightest twitch from the rear of the car as you race through Casino Square and your weekend could be over. It's the most dramatic Saturday on the calendar. As Max Verstappen said after crashing during qualifying in 2023, 'There is no such thing as a low risk lap in Monaco. It doesn't exist if you want to be fast because you have to be on the limit.'

With its warm climate and tax-free living, Monaco has for a long time been home to a whole host of drivers, but when F1 comes to town, it's the home of 'glitz and glamour'. The race attracts some of the biggest celebrities on the planet: J-Lo, Orlando Bloom, Brad Pitt, George Clooney, Will Smith, Neymar, Maria Sharapova and the Williams sisters have all been on the grid. My old producer once told me, 'If you nail your grid walk in Monaco, your work for the year is done!'

MONEY

F1 is a multibillion-pound business that operates at the very highest level, owned by Liberty Media and listed on the NASDAQ. There is a vast amount of money spent within the sport, whether it's making a championship-winning car, jetting the personnel involved around the world, or just the drivers' wages; there's no doubt that F1 is a money business, which we can split it into several categories:

Prize Money

Exactly how much prize money is on offer is a well-kept secret, but it's something we can take an educated guess at. Prize money is roughly 50 per cent of F1's commercial rights profit, so approximately $1.15bn in 2022. How that is split up is another bit of the mystery and history of F1. Ferrari receive a historic payment worth 5 per cent of the prize pot just for taking part in F1 (no other team has competed in every F1 season). The rest of the pot is then divided up based on the previous year's success in the Constructors' Championship, the winner receiving approximately $140m – 14 per cent of the prize pot. This then decreases by around $9m as you go down the order, going down to a mere $60m for tenth place, about 6 per cent of the prize pot.

Cost Cap

Introduced in 2021, the cost cap is a measure designed to level the playing field in F1 and try to deliver a more competitive championship. It means the total budget for a team is limited to $145m per year. The bigger teams have had to trim back how much they spend, with the smaller teams still struggling to find enough cash to spend as much as they are allowed. Driver wages, marketing and the three highest paid members of the team are excluded from the cost cap. Each year every team must go through an audit process, with penalties applied if a team is deemed to have broken the cost cap.

The Bling Factor

F1 is big business, and getting VIPs to come to the race and support 'your' team is an important branding and marketing tool. Teams don't just offer their guests a sandwich and a seat in the grandstand, they spend thousands of pounds giving the biggest names the ultimate experience; they have Michelin-starred chefs cooking their meals, free-flowing drinks, the best view of the paddock and pit lane with a reserved area especially for each team. They have a host of special guests coming to see them throughout the course of the weekend, who get exclusive access to the grid, garage and pit lane: you name it, the wow factor is guaranteed for these VVIPs. It might sound like a money-can't-buy opportunity, but if you've got access to a large amount of money, you can get pretty close to the experience by joining the Paddock Club. In the last few years, this is an area of real growth, and

How to Read F1

you can now pay for a ticket entitling you to be treated to an extra-special experience almost as good as the A-listers.

N is for
ADRIAN NEWEY, NOMEX, LANDO NORRIS and NUTS

ADRIAN NEWEY

Largely regarded as one of the greatest engineers in Formula One, Adrian Newey was born on 26 December 1958 in Stratford-upon-Avon, UK. Newey and his team have produced some of the most aerodynamically efficient cars in F1 history.

He gained a first-class honours degree in Aeronautics and Astronautics from the University of Southampton and immediately began working for the Fittipaldi F1 team and then the March team, where he was successful straight away with two titles in IMSA GTP.

Newey was a race engineer for many a successful driver, mostly in the United States, until he became chief designer at the March team, creating his first F1 car in 1988, the March 881. It wasn't long until Newey became technical director.

A long and successful spell at Williams followed, working alongside Sir Frank Williams and Patrick Head – they became the dominant force in F1 in the early part of the 1990s. The team won the double of constructors' and drivers' titles two years running, with first Nigel Mansell at the wheel (1992) and then Alain Prost (1993).

In 1994 the great Ayrton Senna moved to Williams but it ended in disaster, with Senna's fatal crash at Imola. Newey, along with several other team members, was charged in Italy with manslaughter. The case hung over Newey for years, with appeals and a Supreme Court hearing. He was finally given a full acquittal in May 2005, 11 years after

Adrian Newey

 DID YOU KNOW? Adrian went to school with former *Top Gear* presenter Jeremy Clarkson. They both got expelled from Repton public school at the age of 16.

Senna's tragic death. Newey has since said, 'The honest truth is that no one will ever know exactly what happened. There's no doubt the steering column failed and the big question was whether it failed in the accident or did it cause the accident? There is no question that its design was very poor. However, all the evidence suggests the car did not go off the track as a result of steering column failure.'

A move to McLaren followed at the end of 1996 and he started working for Ron Dennis. Success was to follow, with wins in 1998 and 1999. By the early 2000s rumours were swirling that Newey wanted a change and might step away from F1, but something big was around the corner.

In 2006, Newey signed a multimillion-pound deal to become technical director of Red Bull. It took the team until 2010 to achieve success, but boy, did they achieve success, their rise to domination complete as the team won the constructors' and drivers' titles in 2010, 2011, 2012 and 2013.

When Max Verstappen won the drivers' title in 2021, it was the start of another period of domination for Red Bull, and when the RB19 was created (a car that embraced the new ground-effect rules in F1 so successfully), Red Bull only lost one race of the 2023 season. It was the most dominant season by a team in F1 history.

Newey announced in April 2024 that he would leave Red Bull, ending 18 years with the team. He is a fascinating person, always seen wearing a beaten-up baseball cap, with his dog-eared A4 notebook in hand. He is a very understated man, shying away from the glitz and glamour of F1; his love is for the sheer engineering challenge, and the reward that gives.

NOMEX

This is a fire-resistant, breathable, lightweight, synthetic fibre worn to protect a driver, the wearing of which is compulsory: you must wear Nomex underwear, overalls and balaclava. Gloves are made of two layers of Nomex and soft

leather, while boots are made of Nomex and leather, with rubber soles. All these items must be checked and found to comply with the rules, otherwise a driver could face disqualification.

LANDO NORRIS

Born in Bristol, UK, on 13 November 1999, Lando Norris tried his hand at riding horses and motorbikes before being introduced to karting at the age of seven. He showed a natural aptitude and was soon on the path to becoming a racing driver.

He won the Karting World Championship in 2014, when he was just 14. This was a turning point for Norris; he was signed up by Carlin Motorsport, one of the UK's most respected teams within the junior categories.

Just like Jenson Button and Lewis Hamilton, Norris was awarded the McLaren Autosport BRDC Young Driver Award in 2016, the boss of McLaren saying he was 'a fabulous prospect' and signing him up to the McLaren young driver programme.

A successful season in European Formula 3 followed, where he won his fifth championship title in four years. In 2018, he was beaten to the F2 title by George Russell, but at the end of the season Norris was announced as a McLaren driver, signing a multi-year deal.

Norris got his first podium in 2020 at the Austrian Grand Prix and the following year, McLaren finished 1–2 (the team's first 1–2 since the 2010 Canadian GP) but it was

Daniel Ricciardo standing on the top step. Norris missed out again in Sochi that year when he was in the lead of the race until the rain came and he was outsmarted on strategy.

Norris got his first win in 2024 in Miami, his 110th race for McLaren. A well-timed safety car helped him beat Max Verstappen, but his pace in the second half of the race was rapid, and his win well deserved. His fellow drivers all congratulated him after the race, unusual in F1. It was the feel-good moment of the season. Now, with his first win under his belt, could a championship challenge follow?

Norris has an aggressive driving style and great ultimate pace. Off track he has a 'cheeky chappie' personality and is universally liked by fans and the F1 world.

DID YOU KNOW? Norris holds British and Belgian citizenship (his mum is from Belgium) and he speaks a small amount of Flemish Dutch.

NUTS

No, not the sort that you find in a bar and avoid, and certainly not the ones you find on your own car, these are state-of-the-art nuts that clamp an F1 wheel to the car. Called 'lug nuts', there is one central aluminium or steel locking nut that attaches on and off the axle of the car with a pneumatic air gun. The tech behind these nuts is impressive, with 'floating' nuts now being used, attaching the nut to the wheel, to enable a faster pit stop.

DID YOU KNOW? An F1 wheel nut can cost upwards of £1,000.

O is for
ESTEBAN OCON, OVERSTEER/UNDERSTEER and OVERTAKING

ESTEBAN OCON

Born in Normandy, France, on 17 September 1996, Esteban Ocon currently drives for the Alpine team. He won the Hungary Grand Prix in 2021 and happens to be one of the tallest drivers on the grid at 6ft 1in (186cm). He started karting aged ten, won the European Formula 3 Championship in 2014 and became GP3 champion in 2015, before signing with the Mercedes Junior Team.

Ocon made his F1 debut in 2016 driving for Manor. He's had spells with Force India and Renault (now Alpine). His former karting rival, Pierre Gasly, is his current teammate but it's an awkward relationship, with the pair admitting they will never be best friends.

DID YOU KNOW? Ocon's parents had to sell their family home and his dad's garage to fund their son's karting career. After selling the house, they lived and travelled to races in a caravan, which Ocon also used as his motorhome.

OVERSTEER/UNDERSTEER

You will hear these two terms when a car is trying to corner.

» **Understeer:** When a driver turns the steering wheel, and the car doesn't turn into the corner but continues in a forward motion. This could be due to track conditions or carrying too much speed into the corner.

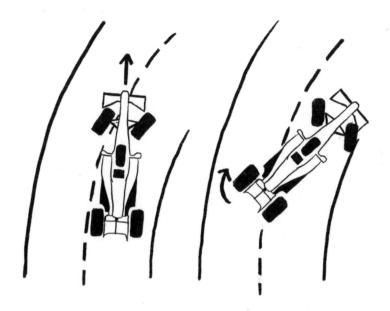

» **Oversteer:** When the momentum of the car breaks its rear tyres' traction. You can see it when the rear of the car rotates towards the front of the car. In simple terms, it's when the rear of the car tries to overtake the front.

OVERTAKING

If you're driving on a motorway or dual-carriageway, overtaking is a simple move that you hardly think about. But try it at 320kph on a racetrack against some of the best drivers in the world, and it becomes a little trickier.

When overtaking on a straight, the attacking driver will tuck themselves in behind the lead car to use their slipstream. The car in front punches a hole in the air, allowing the attacker to have less air resistance, leading to an increase in speed and facilitating a move around them.

Overtaking into a corner, the attacking driver needs to carry more speed, or grip. Remember Hamilton being described as the 'last of the late brakers'? Well, if you manage to brake later than your competitor, you will take that advantage into the corner and can safely pass the car that was in front of you. That is unless you carry too much speed into the corner, which can lead to a potential lock-up, or even a crash.

An off-track overtake happens when the attacking car goes outside track limits while making the manoeuvre. If that occurs, they must give the place back and could face a penalty for violating track limits.

P is for

**PADDOCK, PARC FERMÉ,
SERGIO PÉREZ, OSCAR PIASTRI,
PITS, PIT BOARD, PIT STOPS,
PLANK, PODIUM, POINTS,
POLE POSITION and ALAIN PROST**

PADDOCK

The enclosed area behind the pit garages where the F1 teams have their engineering trucks and hospitality units is known as the paddock. This varies from race to race, but for European races the paddock usually has the same set-up. For fly-aways, the paddock changes as the engineering and hospitality units can't be taken around the world, so permanent structures are used.

PARC FERMÉ

This is a fenced-off area 'off-limits' to anyone apart from race officials. The cars are driven into Parc Fermé after qualifying (and the race). After qualifying the cars are returned to the teams in 'Parc Fermé conditions', meaning the cars can't be changed (with the exception of very minor alterations that have to be made with a scrutineer present).

SERGIO PÉREZ

A Mexican father of four, Pérez has raced for Sauber, McLaren, Force India, Racing Point and Red Bull. A fan favourite, 'Checo' first entered F1 in 2011 (my first year as a pit-lane reporter).

Pérez is known as a bit of a 'tyre whisperer' for his ability to save tyres and go longer than anyone else in a race, a skill he learned from his days karting, which he started to do aged six. He drove first in Mexico and then the US, with the backing of Telmex, a company owned by

Paddock – Sergio Pérez

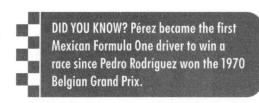

DID YOU KNOW? Pérez became the first Mexican Formula One driver to win a race since Pedro Rodríguez won the 1970 Belgian Grand Prix.

Carlos Slim (the richest person in the world at that time according to *Forbes*).

At the age of 15, Pérez left his home in Guadalajara, buying a one-way ticket to race in the German Formula BMW ADAC series. He lived above the team manager's restaurant for four months, but he couldn't speak German and suffered from homesickness. Pérez stuck it out for two years before moving to Britain. The Ferrari Driver Academy signed Pérez, and at the end of 2010 he was announced as a Sauber driver for the 2011 F1 season. I remember his first podium, a hard-fought second place at the 2012 Malaysian Grand Prix.

A season at McLaren was followed by several years at Force India, which became Racing Point after a buyout by Canadian businessman Lawrence Stroll. By the end of the 2020 season, though, it was clear Pérez would be out of a seat.

Before leaving the team, Pérez won his first F1 race. It was the last race of 2020, in Bahrain. Pérez collided with Charles Leclerc at the start of the race, which saw him tumble down the order to last place, but he fought his way through the field and, with the help of a handily timed safety car, won the race. In a year of Covid chaos, that moment with Pérez standing on his car celebrating a long-awaited win was simply marvellous.

Red Bull picked up Pérez for 2021 to drive alongside Max Verstappen. In 2022, the team won the constructors' title, their first since 2013. The following year, Verstappen and Pérez finished 1–2 in the Drivers' Championship, the first time Red Bull's drivers had ever done that.

OSCAR PIASTRI

This Australian driver grew up in Melbourne, just a stone's throw from Albert Park. One of the youngest drivers in F1, Oscar Jack Piastri was born on 6 April 2001, just a month after Michael Schumacher had won that year's Australian Grand Prix.

After the almost obligatory karting start, he had great success in single-seaters, and signed with the Renault Sport Academy in January 2020. Piastri then won the F3 and F2 titles in consecutive seasons and he soon became the talk of the paddock.

His first time in an F1 car was at a test in Bahrain in 2020. It seemed like his destiny was set when he became the Alpine (the new name for Renault) reserve driver for 2022. Further tests for Alpine and two private tests with McLaren kept Piastri and his management team, including fellow Australian and former F1 driver Mark Webber, busy.

Everyone thought Piastri would drive for Williams in 2023. However, Fernando Alonso, driving for Alpine in 2022, threw the whole paddock into chaos when he announced during the summer break that he would leave the team at the end of the year to go to Aston Martin, Alpine's closest rivals at the time. Alpine immediately put out a statement saying the vacant seat would be filled by their reserve driver, Oscar Piastri ... only no one had told Oscar. They young Aussie took to social media to say that, without his agreement, Alpine had announced him as their driver for next year. He said he had not signed a contract with the team and would not be driving for them in 2023.

It went legal, with Alpine believing Piastri was theirs, but McLaren had other ideas and insisted they had signed the young Australian to drive for them in 2023. The FIA's Contract Recognition Board (CRB), however, made their ruling in Piastri's favour. Alpine had lost their future star driver.

Piastri was unveiled as a McLaren driver at the start of 2023, but the team had missed several key development targets through the winter, leaving Piastri and his teammate, Lando Norris, struggling with the car. However, with a massive in-season development push, Piastri took fourth place at the British Grand Prix, and fifth at the next race in Hungary.

His first podium was at Japan 2023, finishing third, and at the next race in Qatar he won his first race, the sprint race, ahead of his teammate Norris. His rookie year satisfied all the critics and cemented his place in the hearts of the fans, with his mum, Nicole, often taking to social media to lovingly call out her son.

PITS

My second home! This is the area where the cars live and are worked on through the course of a race weekend. The pit wall separates the pits from the racetrack. There is a speed limit imposed at the pit entry line, usually 80kph. Access during live sessions is heavily restricted and only certain media are allowed in.

PIT BOARD

Held out from the pit wall to inform a driver of their race position, the time interval to the car ahead and behind, and the number of laps completed or remaining, pit boards are notoriously hard to see from within a fast-moving F1 car. Before radios were introduced, pit boards were the only way to communicate with a driver. Nowadays, they are used as a back-up.

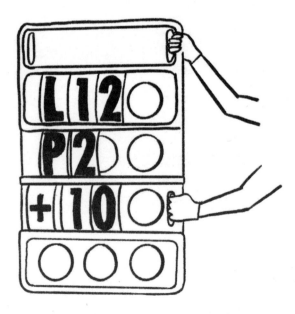

PIT STOPS

The pit stop – when a car comes into the pits and stops outside their garage for either a tyre change or for any work to be carried out on the car – is a vital part of a Grand Prix, giving teams the chance to improve their race position through slick work.

In a scheduled pit stop, a team of 22 mechanics and technicians, made up from both sides of the garage, come together in an almost balletic sequence to change all four tyres on the car in the quickest way possible. The roles are: wheel off, wheel on, and gunner (the person with the wheel gun). There is a front and rear jack operator, a back-up for both, someone to stabilise the car on either side, and two people ready for any front-wing adjustment needed. There are two final roles: 'pit clear', the person that presses the button when all the tyres have been fitted properly and the car is ready to be released, and the traffic controller, who has a button to signal when the pit lane is clear so the driver can drive away safely.

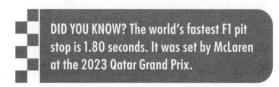

DID YOU KNOW? The world's fastest F1 pit stop is 1.80 seconds. It was set by McLaren at the 2023 Qatar Grand Prix.

PLANK

This is a hard wooden strip, fitted underneath the car, down the middle, used to check whether the car is being run too close to the track surface. If it is, it will be apparent because the wood will be excessively worn.

PODIUM

Usually positioned above the pit lane, this is where the top three drivers stand to receive their trophies, where the national anthems of the winning driver and team are played, and where the Champagne is sprayed.

POINTS

Points in F1 have been awarded since the World Championship began – but how many points on offer has varied greatly over the years (and at the time of writing there are proposals for them to change again for 2025). Most recently, the sprint race, held on the day before the main race at selected grands prix, has seen more points awarded across an F1 weekend. The points awarded for the 2024 season are as follows:

- » The winner of a Grand Prix gets 25 points
- » Second place = 18 points
- » Third = 15 points
- » Fourth = 12 points
- » Fifth = 10 points
- » Sixth = 8 points

- » Seventh = 6 points
- » Eighth = 4 points
- » Ninth = 2 points
- » Tenth = 1 point

There is also a point on offer if you set the fastest lap of the race (as long as you finish within the top ten). The top eight finishers in the sprint race, of which six were scheduled for 2024, are awarded fewer points: eight for the winner, down to one for eighth place.

All the points scored by the two drivers from a team are added together to make the constructors' standings.

POLE POSITION

The place at the front of the starting grid, awarded to the driver who sets the fastest lap time in qualifying.

ALAIN PROST

A French Formula One four-times World Champion, Prost was interested in sport from an early age and thought about becoming a footballer (breaking his nose several times in the process), but luckily for everyone, he started karting at 14 and fell in love with motorsport. He quicky progressed up the ladder, tuning engines to raise extra money for his racing. He won in karting, then Formula Renault and finally Formula 3. He had several options to join F1 teams but finally chose McLaren in 1980. He soon became disillusioned with results as they suffered reliability issues and mechanical failures, and, despite having a two-year contract, he dramatically left and signed for Renault.

His first F1 win was at his home race, the French Grand Prix of 1981, in Dijon. It opened the floodgates and changed Prost's mindset: 'Before, you thought you could do it. Now you know you can.'

But while Prost kept winning, a championship was elusive, and a war of words developed between Renault and their

driver, with Prost saying the car was not competitive. His contract was terminated prematurely at the end of 1983 and Prost returned to McLaren.

In 1984, alongside Niki Lauda, the pair drove the John Barnard-designed McLaren MP4/2, one of the most loved cars of the decade. Prost lost the title to Lauda that year by half a point, the closest losing margin in F1 history.

Finally, in 1985, Prost won the first of his four World Championships. He won again in 1986, becoming the first driver to successfully defend an F1 title since Jack Brabham in 1960. But 1988 saw Ayrton Senna join McLaren and the now infamous rivalry was set in motion. Prost, nicknamed 'The Professor' for his astute analysis of a race and his rivals, had a very different driving style to that of Senna, which was much more instinctual. This led to one of the greatest battles in F1 history, with Prost accusing Senna of 'dangerous driving'. Prost versus Senna converted millions of people into F1 fans. The two warred their way through the late 1980s and early 90s, including a notorious crash between the pair at the Japanese GP in 1989 that decided the title in Prost's favour.

The two could not continue in the same team and in 1990, Ferrari signed Prost to partner Nigel Mansell. However, Prost and Senna continued their fight on track and, again, the title went down to the penultimate race of the season, once again in Japan. At the first corner, Senna drove his car into Prost's Ferrari, taking them both out of the race. It was one of the most controversial moves in F1 history. Prost ended the season seven points adrift of Senna.

After falling out with Ferrari in 1991 and having his contract terminated early, Prost took a year out before signing for Williams for the 1993 season alongside promoted test driver Damon Hill. It was a season that saw Prost lift his fourth and final title before announcing his retirement. The final podium of his career saw him stand alongside his great rival Ayrton Senna in Adelaide, and two of the greatest rivals in the sport's history embraced. It was a fitting end to a racing career, and rivalry, that defined the 1980s and 90s.

After Senna's death, Prost was a pallbearer at his funeral. He has said that when Senna died, 'I felt a part of me had died also because our careers had been so bound together.'

QUALIFYING

This is the part of the race weekend where the drivers see who can set the best time for one lap around the circuit, and it decides the order the cars will line up on race day.

The first part, called Q1, lasts for 18 minutes and features all 20 drivers, but the 5 drivers who set the slowest times get knocked out, leaving just 15 to go through to the second part of qualifying. Q2 lasts for 15 minutes and sees the top 15 drivers try and set the best time they can. Again, 5 get knocked out, with only the top 10 proceeding to the final part of qualifying, Q3.

In Q3, with 12 minutes on the clock, the remaining 10 drivers try again to set the fastest time. In dry conditions, each driver usually does an out lap, a fast lap and an in lap. They will have the time and tyres to do this process twice during Q3. Depending on how many tyres the driver has left, they will try and use a new set of the fastest/softest tyres to do those runs. The more the circuit is used, the more rubber is laid down from the tyres, meaning the conditions tend to get faster and faster. At the end of Q3, the track is normally at its fastest, so the ideal lap will usually be set right at the end of this session. The driver setting the fastest time will start in 'pole position' at the front of the grid.

R is for

RACE DIRECTOR, RAIN, RECORDS, RED BULL, RETIREMENTS, DANIEL RICCIARDO, RIDE HEIGHT, RIVALS, NICO ROSBERG and GEORGE RUSSELL

How to Read F1

RACE DIRECTOR

This entry could have come under W, for Charlie Whiting, who was the first race director I met in F1, and the most extraordinary man. He loved F1 and was part of the Brabham team, run by a certain Bernie Ecclestone, during the 1970s and 80s.

Let me tell you what a race director *officially* does. They oversee a race weekend, making decisions regarding safety and other race-related issues. They work closely with the stewards to make sure that any incident or rules that may have been broken are investigated and resolved as quickly and as fairly as possible. They also have the authority to stop a race or race weekend. They produce the race director's notes, which are circuit-specific additions to the rules, and hold a drivers' briefing after the first practice sessions, which is attended by all the drivers and key personnel.

Whiting was also the safety delegate, head of the F1 technical department, and the official race starter. He managed to juggle all these roles impeccably, feeding into Bernie Ecclestone and the FIA with a respected authority. He also made time to speak to the media, acting as a conduit for his employers, the FIA and FOM (Formula One Management). At the start of every season, Whiting would hold a media briefing explaining any new rules, processes and safety features. Traditionally this was held in the Australian press conference room and could last for over an hour. It was a fascinating insight into how the new season would be run.

It's important to remember a race director is responsible for the safe running of an event. This means if there is an incident during a race weekend, they will lead the investigation.

Whiting's door was always open if you had a question. He was controlled and dignified, quite something with so many personalities to balance. The drivers and teams, the FIA, and Ecclestone's FOM all highly respected Whiting. It was a shock to the whole paddock when he died ahead of the Australian GP in 2019, aged just 66.

Since his death, his roles have been split up and distributed among several people; it was just too much for one person. Michael Masi was the first race director after Whiting's death, and Niels Wittich is the current race director.

RAIN

Unlike Wimbledon, or the Arthur Ashe Stadium in the US, there is no canopy to cover a Grand Prix and rain doesn't often stop play in F1. In fact, there was a time when Bernie Ecclestone spoke about his desire to have a 'rain button' that he could press at any time he liked to 'spice up a dull race'.

As a pit-lane reporter, I cannot tell you the number of times I've been soaked by rain, and yes, it does liven things up, but it can also cause delays, and sometimes even the postponement or cancellation of a race weekend.

Rain has given us some amazing races, and drivers who excel in wet conditions are referred to as 'rain-masters'.

Max Verstappen, Lewis Hamilton and Jenson Button (who won the longest and wettest race in F1 history in Canada in 2011) are all 'rain-masters'.

In 1993, at the European Grand Prix in Donington, UK, Ayrton Senna drove 'the lap of the gods' in the pouring rain in what legendary commentator Murray Walker described as astounding. In addition to this, Michael Schumacher at the Spanish Grand Prix in 1996, Jim Clark at the 1963 Belgium GP, Lewis Hamilton at Silverstone in 2008 and Damon Hill at the 1994 Japanese Grand Prix at Suzuka are just some of my favourite performances in the rain.

RECORDS

Records are there to be broken in F1, so anything I write now could be obsolete by the time you read this. However, there are some records that are highly unlikely to be broken and I feel it's safe to write about these (have I jinxed it now?).

» The oldest driver to start an F1 race is a record that goes to Monégasque driver Louis Chiron. He competed in his home race, the 1955 Monaco Grand Prix, at the age of 55 years and 292 days. Now, despite Fernando Alonso and Lewis Hamilton racing into their forties, I don't think even they will be taking that record away from Chiron.

» Conversely, Max Verstappen (who holds many F1 records) is the youngest driver to ever start an F1 race. He was just 17 years and 166 days when he first drove for Toro Rosso (Red Bull's 'second' team) in 2015.

Rain – Records

It was a controversial decision by Red Bull, with many people saying Verstappen was too young and lacked experience. (Max certainly had the last laugh there!) However, in 2016 the FIA changed the regulations, setting a minimum age of 18 to race in F1, meaning Verstappen will always be the youngest driver to race in F1 (unless the rules change again).

» Verstappen also holds the record of the youngest driver to win an F1 race, winning the 2016 Spanish Grand Prix aged 18 years, 228 days. The records for Verstappen also include the youngest person to score points, set the fastest lap and to achieve a grand slam.

» Italian driver Andrea de Cesaris suffered 18 consecutive retirements and holds the record for the greatest number of DNFs (did not finishes) in F1 history, with a total of 148 retirements in his career.

» The record for the closest qualifying session was first set in Jerez in 1997 when three drivers set exactly the same time. Not even a thousandth of a second separated Michael Schumacher's Ferrari and the two Williams of Heinz-Harald Frentzen and Jacques Villeneuve, who all set a time of 1.21.072. Grid positions were awarded in the order the times were set, so Villeneuve, setting his time first, was on pole, Schumacher second, Frentzen third. That record was equalled at qualifying for the Canadian Grand Prix in 2024 as George Russell and Max Verstappen both set a time of 1.12.000. Russell was awarded pole by virtue of setting his time before Verstappen.

RED BULL

This is one of the newest teams in F1, founded in 2005, essentially as a marketing tool for Red Bull energy drinks. Dietrich Mateschitz bought the Jaguar team for one dollar (and then invested $400m over the next three years) and the Red Bull team was born. Mateschitz's friend and confidant, Helmut Marko, enlisted Christian Horner as team principal and the pair poached top designer Adrian Newey from McLaren, then set about winning a world title.

Sebastian Vettel gave Red Bull a first race victory at the Chinese Grand Prix in 2009. It took a further year for the team to win the drivers' and constructors' world titles, which they dominated between 2010 and 2013 with Vettel and Mark Webber. They have returned to winning ways again with Max Verstappen and Sergio Pérez, dominating F1 since 2022.

In October 2022, Mateschitz passed away. Since his death, while the team and Verstappen continue to win on track, off track a power vacuum has grown, and in April 2024 Newey announced he would be leaving Red Bull. The future success of the team now seems a little more uncertain.

RETIREMENTS

This term is used to describe a car which drops out of a race. In the current era, mechanical retirements are much rarer than they used to be because F1 cars now are more reliable. At the start of the 2024 season, for the first time in F1 history, there were no retirements in the opening race of the season.

The race with the most retirements statistically was the 1996 Monaco Grand Prix, when 85.7 per cent of the field didn't finish the race (18 of the 21 starters). The race was run in pouring-wet conditions, the first time it had rained all weekend. To say it was crash-tastic is an understatement. By the fifth lap only 13 racers remained in the Grand Prix. A crash near the end of the race saw another three cars wiped out, which left only Olivier Panis,

David Coulthard and Johnny Herbert to take the chequered flag. It was Panis's first and only F1 victory.

DANIEL RICCIARDO

With his famous smile and enigmatic personality, it's no real surprise that Daniel Ricciardo is a favourite with fans wherever he goes in the world. Born in Perth, Australia, to Italian-Australian parents, Ricciardo started karting aged nine and in 2007, while racing in Italy, he was signed up by Red Bull's Junior Team.

Daniel stepped up to the Formula Renault 3.5 Series in 2010, where he missed out on the title by just two points. It was an impressive debut. He was also reserve and test driver for Red Bull and Toro Rosso and drove at the end-of-season test. He impressed Christian Horner, setting a lap 1.3 seconds faster than Sebastian Vettel had done in qualifying for the Abu Dhabi GP.

Ricciardo signed for minnows Hispania Racing in 2011, before spending two years at Toro Rosso, until he got the call from Red Bull to replace his fellow countryman, Mark Webber.

He started well, with a podium at his home race. However, his car was later disqualified, a great shame as it was the first time an Australian had stood on his home podium. He won his first points for Red Bull at the 2014 Spanish GP and achieved his first win in Canada. He went on to win two more races that year.

Retirements – Daniel Ricciardo

For me, Daniel's most memorable win at Red Bull was his redemption race at Monaco 2018, overturning the painful memories of 2016, when he lost the race with a slow pit stop. It was of course celebrated with a shoey (where Ricciardo famously drinks Champagne from his sweaty race shoe) and a swan dive into the Red Bull pool on top of their floating motorhome.

In the summer of 2018, Ricciardo announced he would leave Red Bull to join Renault in a mega-bucks move worth a reported $30m a year. It was a move that shocked the whole paddock, as no one expected him to walk away from the team that had backed him since 2007. Christian Horner was so surprised by Ricciardo's decision that he initially thought his driver was joking when he phoned him to say that he was switching to Renault. Daniel later outlined his thinking: 'I took a little bit of a gamble on myself […] I felt like I needed a change and I needed to kind of just remove myself a bit.'

A couple of relatively fruitless years with the French team followed that failed to deliver the championship-winning car that Ricciardo wanted; he scored just two podiums in his time with Renault. Ricciardo joined McLaren in 2021 and got his first win in over three years at Monza as he led the team home to a 1–2. A fitting win for the man with such rich Italian heritage and, you guessed it, a shoey was the celebration. However, his time at McLaren came to an end after two years and Ricciardo found himself without a seat.

Ricciardo was again seeking redemption and chose to rejoin Red Bull for 2023 as their third driver, a term not used in F1 circles for many years as there are only two cars, and two drivers able to compete. Ricciardo spent time in the simulator and promoting Red Bull, and soon found himself back racing in F1 with the junior team, taking the seat of Nyck de Vries for the second part of the 2023 season. However, a heavy crash at the Dutch GP saw Ricciardo out with a broken metacarpal bone in his hand and he missed the next four races.

Ricciardo stayed with the junior team for 2024 but his motivation is winning a place back with Red Bull.

DID YOU KNOW? Ricciardo's nickname, in a reference to his racing style, is the honey badger, which may look cute and cuddly but is known for its strength, ferocity and fearlessness!

RIDE HEIGHT

This refers to the height difference between the underside of the car (called the floor) and the track surface. Generally, the lower this is, the better the car performs.

RIVALS

There have been some epic rivalries in F1. These titanic duels of the tarmac, two drivers going toe-to-toe with each other while setting the time sheets on fire, are what grip us F1 fans and make F1 the pinnacle of motorsport. Think about the greatest rivalries in F1: Senna vs Prost, Lauda vs Hunt, Schumacher vs Hill and Häkkinen, and Hamilton vs Rosberg and then Verstappen. These were great sporting rivalries on track, that nearly always spilled to off-track shenanigans. While there is great respect between drivers, certainly in the duos above, there was no love lost between them.

These are my personal top three rivalries:

Senna vs Prost – 1985–94

In a well-documented rivalry, Prost and Senna went head-to-head numerous times on track. It was all-consuming as these men battled for world titles. They managed 7 championships between them and 92 race wins. The rivalry began in earnest when the two drivers raced alongside each other at McLaren in 1988. Prost was a double World Champion and, at first, was keen to race alongside this 'new talent'. However, that harmony didn't last long and in 1989 the gentlemen's agreement not to overtake on the first lap of the San Marino GP was reneged on by Senna, which led to all-out war between the two. While it was great to watch (and it was the thing that made me fall in love with F1), for the drivers it was an exhausting battle that endured until Senna's untimely death in 1994.

Lauda vs Hunt – 1975–7

If you haven't seen the film *Rush*, directed by Ron Howard, it tells the story better than I can, but these two giants of motorsport went head-to-head on the Grand Prix circuit for three magical years. They came through the junior ranks together and lived with each other before 'making it' in F1. The rivalry came to a head in 1976 in one of F1's most dramatic World Championship fights, with Hunt and Lauda both feeding off the controversy of that year. Hunt was disqualified from races, then reinstated, and Lauda was on fine form, winning four of the first six races that year. However, disaster struck at the Nürburgring when Lauda crashed, and his car was engulfed in fire. The near-fatal crash only made Lauda want the title more, and he made an incredible comeback at the Italian Grand Prix, just 40 days after his accident. The championship went down to the wire in Japan, but Lauda thought the conditions were too dangerous to race in and retired, leaving Hunt to take the title. Lauda bounced back in 1977 and retirement beckoned for Hunt, but it was a thrilling rivalry that will live in F1 folklore forever.

Hamilton vs Rosberg – 2013–16

I was lucky enough to report on this amazing rivalry that took one man right to the limit. Hamilton had a natural, instinctive talent behind the wheel of an F1 car and he had won his first world title with McLaren in 2008, before moving to Mercedes in 2013. Rosberg had been at the team for much longer, but in 2014, with the regulation changes, he suddenly found himself in a potentially championship-winning car. Rosberg started 2014 well, winning the first race of the season, setting himself up for a title challenge. He and Hamilton went toe-to-toe in Bahrain, almost dancing around the desert, so nimble were their racing moves. It was beautiful and thrilling to watch as the Silver Arrows duked it out under the floodlights. Hamilton took the win, but as the season progressed, the temperature in the team was rising – during qualifying for the Monaco GP, Rosberg was investigated and later cleared for running off the track on purpose to bring out the yellow flags and destroy any chance Hamilton had of getting pole.

Hamilton went on to win the title that year, and the following year, but it all came to blows (in a very Prost vs Senna way) in 2016, at the Spanish Grand Prix. The two drivers started alongside each other, Hamilton on pole, Rosberg next to him. The two battled from the start but only managed to make it to turn 4 before wiping each other out. I can't begin to tell you about the levels of drama in the paddock as soon as the journalists and broadcasters realised what had happened. Neither Hamilton nor Rosberg would accept blame for the crash (the stewards deemed it a racing incident).

The battle continued all season, with another clash between the two in Austria. It went all the way to the final race of the season, under the floodlights of Abu Dhabi. Hamilton started on pole and did all he could to win the championship by winning the race, but Rosberg finished in second place and won his first world title by five points.

Rosberg really did give it everything that year, and at the end of the season he surprised the whole of the F1 world by announcing his immediate retirement from the sport.

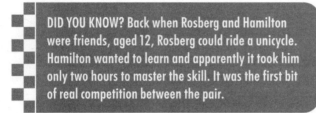

DID YOU KNOW? Back when Rosberg and Hamilton were friends, aged 12, Rosberg could ride a unicycle. Hamilton wanted to learn and apparently it took him only two hours to master the skill. It was the first bit of real competition between the pair.

NICO ROSBERG

Nico Erik Rosberg, 2016 World Champion, was born in Wiesbaden, West Germany, in 1985, and is the only child of Gesine and Keke Rosberg, the Finn who won the F1 title in 1982. Nico raced under the German flag, representing his mother's birth country.

He lives in Monaco (his family moved from West Germany when Nico was just four weeks old). He speaks five languages fluently and excelled in maths and science at school. Rosberg started driving when he was just four, steering a car while sitting on his dad's lap. He started competing at six, and grew up on the karting scene with Lewis Hamilton, both driving for Keke Rosberg's team.

A successful junior career followed and, after winning GP2 in 2005, Rosberg signed a five-year deal with Williams, scoring points on his debut in 2006 and achieving two podiums in 2008. Rosberg signed with Mercedes in 2010 to partner first Michael Schumacher and then Lewis Hamilton, and won the 2016 F1 World Championship.

Rosberg is possibly the cleverest, wiliest and most studious driver I've ever met in F1. He analyses the races, has a keen grasp of engineering, and an unnerving ability to answer an interview question with just one word. Since his retirement at the end of 2016, Rosberg has become a broadcaster and uses his knowledge of F1 to ask brilliantly direct questions to drivers and team bosses, helping viewers better understand the racing and politics of F1.

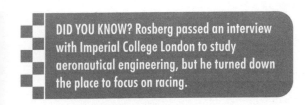

DID YOU KNOW? Rosberg passed an interview with Imperial College London to study aeronautical engineering, but he turned down the place to focus on racing.

GEORGE RUSSELL

George William Russell was born on 15 February 1998 in King's Lynn, Norfolk. The youngest of three children, Russell started karting aged seven alongside his brother, Benjy. He became MSA British Champion in 2009 before winning a string of titles in the junior categories.

Russell's path to F1 started when he was just 15. He arranged a meeting with Toto Wolff, hoping the Austrian businessman would become his manager. He walked into the meeting dressed in a black suit that was two sizes too small for him, holding a laptop that contained his prized PowerPoint presentation. 'It was well made, although he was a bit nervous. He also looked a little more like an accountant than a racing driver,' Toto Wolff remembered. But his dedication to racing was unquestionable and Wolff signed him up, beginning his career-long association with Mercedes.

Russell became the fourth driver to win consecutive GP3 and GP2 titles, after Lewis Hamilton, Nico Hulkenberg and Charles Leclerc. In October 2018, it was announced that he had signed a multi-year deal with Williams – but the car of 2019 was far removed from the winning Williams of the 1990s.

Russell scored his first F1 points in 2020, but it also saw him make the 'biggest mistake of [his] career' as he crashed out from tenth place when following the safety car. I still remember the images of him at Imola, sat down on the grass behind a crash-barrier, crying with frustration. Those first points came when he got the chance to drive in a Mercedes F1 car that year in the Sakhir GP, replacing Lewis Hamilton who had Covid. No pressure then! He missed out on pole by just 0.026 seconds. Russell could have won the race but for a mistake in the pits and an unfortunate puncture. He finished ninth and scored a point for the fastest lap, but it should have been more. Again, Russell was crying – we were all crying.

George Russell

Russell finally got the call from Toto Wolff to replace Valtteri Bottas for the 2022 season alongside Lewis Hamilton. His first podium came at the Australian Grand Prix, where he finished third, his first pole position was at the Hungarian GP that year, and he took his maiden victory at Interlagos in Brazil, winning both the sprint race and the Grand Prix.

Russell is a director of the Grand Prix Drivers' Association and frequently speaks out on behalf of the drivers in F1. It was a position he was elected to by his peers and shows the respect he has garnered within F1 circles.

DID YOU KNOW? During lockdown, Russell lived at his parents' house, along with his sister's family. His trainer also moved in because George wanted to stay in peak physical condition for when F1 resumed.

S is for
CARLOS SAINZ,
LOGAN SARGEANT, SAUBER,
MICHAEL SCHUMACHER,
SECTORS, AYRTON SENNA,
SILVERSTONE, SIMs, GUENTHER
STEINER, STEWARDS,
SIR JACKIE STEWART,
STRATEGY and LANCE STROLL

CARLOS SAINZ

Carlos Sainz (aka The Smooth Operator) is a Spanish F1 driver who takes after his father, Carlos Sainz Sr (El Matador), a double World Rally Champion. Sainz Jr was born in Madrid on 1 September 1994; his father has mentored him all the way from karting to F1.

Sainz started karting aged eight and after great success moved into single-seaters. He was picked up by Red Bull and their junior programme in 2010 and went on to win the Formula Renault 3.5 Series Championship in 2014. He was rewarded with a young driver test in the Red Bull car and impressed. Sainz was announced as a Toro Rosso driver for the 2015 season, partnering fellow rookie Max Verstappen.

After nearly four years at Toro Rosso, Sainz moved to Renault and then McLaren, and when Sebastian Vettel left Ferrari it was Sainz who, surprisingly, got the call to replace him. He would partner Charles Leclerc from 2021 but the team were uncompetitive that year.

In 2022 Sainz won his first F1 race, the British Grand Prix, his 150th race in F1. I remember him being applauded into the media pen at Silverstone; everyone was delighted for the Spaniard, who I believe remains one of the most underrated drivers of his time.

The following year he won again under the floodlights at the Singapore Grand Prix, a season dominated by Max Verstappen. It was an impressive showing, Sainz using his years of racing knowledge to stay in front of his rivals. He was the only non-Red Bull driver to win a race in 2023.

Sainz was expected to stay with Ferrari, until Lewis Hamilton was suddenly announced to be signing for the team from 2025. The news meant the Spaniard was out of a seat at the end of the year, but would continue to race for the team in 2024.

Appendicitis meant Sainz had to be replaced at the last minute for the Bahrain GP, the second round of the 2024 season. He made a rapid recovery, though, and despite still wearing bandages over his scar, he was cleared to enter the next race. Incredibly, just two weeks after his appendectomy, Sainz started from the front row of the grid and won the Australian GP. In July 2024, Sainz announced that he had signed a long-term deal with Williams, his fifth team in Formula One.

DID YOU KNOW? Before signing for Ferrari, Sainz drove a VW Golf that his parents got him for his 18th birthday. He now has a custom-made Ferrari 812 Competizione that features carpets with his 55 race number emblazed on them.

LOGAN SARGEANT

Logan Hunter Sargeant is a rare thing, an American F1 driver. As America has seen a huge growth in F1 interest, it was only a matter of time before they had a driver on the grid. Logan was born in Fort Lauderdale, Florida, on 31 December 2000. His elder brother Dalton has competed in NASCAR.

After karting and single-seater success, Sargeant was backed by Williams and was announced as an F1 driver for the team for 2023. He scored his only point that year at the USA Grand Prix in Austin, to great celebration from the team and fans alike. Despite rumours Sargeant would lose his seat, new boss James Vowles backed the American for the 2024 campaign, but it would prove to be his last for Williams.

SAUBER

Founded by Peter Sauber, this is one of the oldest brands in F1. In 1986, Sauber's car won the Nürburgring 1000km race and gained an exceptional reputation within F1, partnering some of the biggest names in the sport: Red Bull, Ferrari, Ford and BMW.

In 2026, Audi will take over the Sauber F1 team. Former McLaren team principal Andreas Seidl, in his role as CEO, will oversee the transition.

MICHAEL SCHUMACHER

Seven times World Champion, Michael Schumacher is one of the most successful racing drivers of all time.

He was born in Hürth, West Germany, on 3 January 1969, to parents Rolf and Elisabeth. His father was a bricklayer who went on to run the local karting track, while his mother worked in the track's canteen. Schumacher started karting at four and was the youngest member of the Kerpen-Horrem kart club. He won his first club championship aged just six.

By 1987, as German and European karting champion, Schumacher decided school wasn't for him, so he quit and became a mechanic. No wonder he was so adept at tuning a car and giving technical feedback. By 1990, Schumacher had joined the Mercedes-Benz junior racing programme and raced in the World Sportscar Championship. It was an unusual way into F1.

He had his first test in an F1 car in 1991 and was so impressive he was racing just a week later for the Jordan-Ford team. Jordan's then designer, and one of my favourite people to work with, Gary Anderson, told me that the first time Schumacher jumped into an F1 car 'we all thought he was trying too hard and over the limit. [When we] said that to him, he just looked at us with a smile and said, "No, I'm well under the limit, I just need to feel the car." We were all just very, very impressed.'

Schumacher's first Grand Prix was in Spa-Francorchamps, where the German media were delighted when he qualified in seventh place. However, he was forced to retire the car on the first lap, suffering from a clutch issue. He went on to race with Benetton for the rest of that year, scoring his first points. In 1992, Schumacher got his first F1 podium at the Mexican Grand Prix and won his first race at a wet Belgium GP. On winning his first world title in 1994, the year Ayrton Senna died, he dedicated the title to the Brazilian. More wins and world titles followed, as well as plenty of collisions and controversy.

Ferrari and Schumacher became the dominant force in F1 in 2000–4. Schumacher was astounding, clinical, controversial, and seemingly unstoppable. So good was he that in 2002, on his way to a fifth championship, he won 11 of the 17 races and took the title with 6 races to go. The following year, Schumacher broke Fangio's 46-year record of five Drivers' Championships in winning the drivers' title for the sixth time. In 2004, he won his seventh drivers' world title and a sixth consecutive Constructors' Championship for Ferrari.

Schumacher was fastidious about everything. He was the first driver to bring high-calibre fitness training and diet into his regime – now a 'must' for all drivers, even in the junior categories.

I only met Schumacher after his legendary time with Ferrari had come to an end, and he was driving for the team he had first signed with when he was just a teen, Mercedes. His steely eyes and perfect posture, his no-nonsense approach to interviews and attention to detail were spellbinding. He retired from the sport at the end of 2012, but my time interviewing this F1 great was always an enjoyable and unforgettable experience.

On 29 December 2013, while skiing off-piste with his son (Mick, 14 at the time), Schumacher crashed and suffered a severe brain injury. I remember being at Heathrow, about to check in for a flight to Canada, when my phone started ringing. It didn't stop for the next three hours. The world wanted to know what had happened, what would happen next and, most importantly, would Michael survive? It was a surreal day as news started to come in from Grenoble; he had been airlifted to hospital, operated on, and put into an induced coma. Schumacher was always a private man away from the track and that privacy has continued to this day. He has not been seen in public since the accident.

DID YOU KNOW? Michael Schumacher was the first driver to use a scooter in the paddock, long before Lewis Hamilton. He found it a quicker way to get about and it helped him navigate through the fans.

SECTORS

Each lap is split up into sectors, each roughly a third of the lap. These are officially known as sectors 1, 2 and 3, and help to tell everyone where a car or incident is.

AYRTON SENNA

Words won't do this entry justice or even go halfway to summing up how important Ayrton Senna was to the F1 world. Quite frankly, he was the GOAT.

He was born on 21 March 1960 in São Paulo, Brazil, to a wealthy family descended from Italian immigrants. At the age of four he developed an interest in cars and motor racing and first learned to drive a jeep at his family's farm aged seven. By the age of 13, Senna was racing at Interlagos (the track used for F1) in karting competitions and started his first race in pole position.

How to Read F1

By 1981, Senna had moved to England to begin his single-seater career in a Formula Ford, racing for the Van Diemen team. However, his parents were keen for the 21-year-old to return to Brazil and work in the family business. Duly, he flew back to São Paulo, retiring from racing, but the offer of a seat in Formula Ford 2000, and a pay cheque of £10,000, was enough to reverse that decision.

By 1983, Senna had tested for Williams, Brabham, McLaren and Toleman; he ended up signing with Toleman for the 1984 season. The following year, he moved to Lotus, winning his first F1 race, the 1985 Portuguese Grand Prix.

McLaren's Ron Dennis made his move for Senna at the end of 1987. It was a successful partnership and in 1988 Senna won his first world title. On his way to the title, he put in arguably one of the best qualifying performances of all time in Monaco. He said afterwards, 'I suddenly realised that I was no longer driving the car consciously. I was kind of driving it by instinct, only I was in a different dimension.'

Like many of the greatest drivers, Senna could be ruthless and single-minded on track, leading to many controversial incidents. He was beaten to the title the following year by his fiercest rival and teammate Alain Prost in their final year together at McLaren. The Brazilian won his second title in 1990 and became the youngest consecutive champion in 1991, also becoming the youngest ever three-time World Champion.

Senna moved to the Williams team in 1994 but it would end in tragedy, with Senna's fatal crash at Imola on 1 May.

Ayrton Senna

DID YOU KNOW? Senna was born Ayrton Senna da Silva, but da Silva is the most common surname in Brazil, so he decided to use his mother's maiden name, Senna, when he started racing.

Everyone knows where they were that day, one of the saddest weekends in racing history.

Rubens Barrichello had crashed badly on the Friday; the FIA medical doctor Professor Sid Watkins saved his life after finding him unconscious and struggling to breathe. The following day, Roland Ratzenberger suffered a fatal crash during qualifying. Senna visited the medical centre and Professor Watkins, a great friend of Ayrton, reportedly advised him to walk away from the sport and take up fishing, but Senna was born to race and got back in the car the following day. It would be his last. He was leading the San Marino GP when his Williams crashed heavily into a concrete barrier. Watkins attended the scene and tried to save Senna's life, but he was pronounced dead at 6.40pm local time.

Senna was given a state funeral, the country mourning the loss of their hero. Over half a million people lined the streets of São Paulo, and over 200,000 people filed past his body as it lay in state. The funeral was attended by family and friends, but also by the world of F1: Emerson Fittipaldi, Alain Prost and Sir Jackie Stewart were among the pallbearers. Senna's grave is at the Morumbi cemetery in São Paulo, not far from Interlagos. It's a pilgrimage most people in the F1 paddock make at least once in their career, to pay their respects to one of the greatest.

How to Read F1

Senna's attention to detail, his outstanding technical feedback, his dedication to his physical conditioning, his appeal to the masses, and his charitable trust, made him stand out both in F1 and in the wider world.

SILVERSTONE

This converted World War Two airstrip and pig farm is now home to the British Grand Prix thanks to the Royal Automobile Club, who chose the site in Northampton to bring international motor racing to the UK. With iconic names from villages and towns nearby such as Maggots, Becketts, Stowe, Abbey and Luffield, Silverstone is at the heart of the motorsport movement in the UK.

Now owned by the British Racing Drivers' Club, it's 5.891km long, with 18 turns, and has witnessed some magical

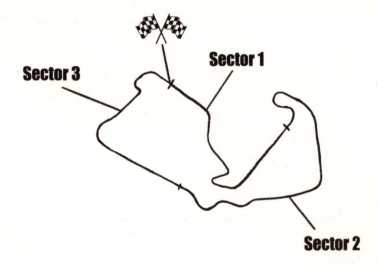

moments in F1 history: Sir Jackie Stewart winning his first British Grand Prix in 1969; Williams with its first ever GP victory in 1979; and Lewis Hamilton romping home in the rain in 2008, winning by more than a minute.

DID YOU KNOW? In 1950, with King George VI in attendance, the first Formula One championship race took place at Silverstone. It was won by Italian driver Giuseppe Farina for Alfa Romeo.

SIMs

Costing millions of pounds, SIMs (or simulators) are a key tool in F1, helping train new drivers, develop a car, and set up the car. Every F1 team has one, with Ferrari recently spending over $1.3m on their state-of-the-art DMG-1 simulator.

SIMs are 'virtual' cars, that allow any driver to drive hundreds of laps around any circuit in the world. Essentially, they are made up of a chassis, which is attached to electromechanical actuators and controlled by powerful computers, and a curved 180-degree projection screen in front of the chassis. This allows the driver to use the steering wheel and pedals as they would in an actual F1 car, to simulate the acceleration, braking and lateral forces that they would feel if they were on track. It's a bit like a gaming console you play at home, but these are high-tech pieces of kit that can replicate the tiniest detail within an F1 car.

How to Read F1

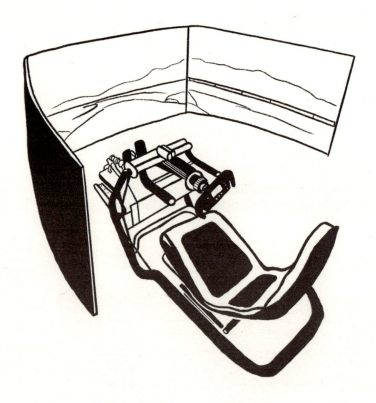

Each team will prepare for a race weekend by using their SIM to find out how to best set up their car. This gives them their 'base' set-up, which they will run on the real racetrack, with the real F1 car, in Free Practice 1.

As the drivers are doing their practice sessions at the track, the SIM driver back at base will jump into the SIM and complete hundreds more laps. Their engineers can make rapid set-up changes so a driver can feel how the mechanical and aerodynamic modifications affect the car.

The SIM team, comprising engineers and the driver, will remotely listen and contribute to all the feedback sessions at the track and form an invaluable test bed for the continued refining of the car across the weekend.

After a race, the SIM will again do its work as the team review its weekend and fine-tune the correlation between the car and the SIM. It's an important process for the team to understand any opportunities they may have missed.

With F1 testing limited, the use of SIMs is vital. The SIM will be used to test developments the team are working on. It runs hand in hand with CFD and wind-tunnel time but, crucially, SIM time is unlimited. It's no wonder the F1 simulator room is one of the busiest rooms in an F1 factory.

DID YOU KNOW? SIM drivers can drive up to 170 laps between Free Practice 2 and 3 (usually overnight on Friday) to help the team figure out which direction to take to set the car up. These sessions take place in whatever time zone the trackside team are in, so SIM crews often work very unsociable hours.

GUENTHER STEINER

The former Haas Team Principal is known for his colourful language on the hit show *Drive to Survive*. The Italian came to F1 via rallying, where he was a mechanic for over a decade, working with the likes of Carlos Sainz Sr and the late, great Colin McRae.

Niki Lauda hand-picked Steiner to come and work for his Jaguar Racing team as managing director. He moved to work with Red Bull as their technical operations director before setting up base in the US. It was there he and Gene Haas started thinking about Haas F1, and Steiner was appointed team principal.

What the team lacked in success on the track, Steiner made up for with his off-track antics. He was perfectly placed when Netflix came into the paddock in 2018. *Drive to Survive* had no pulling power with the big teams in F1, so went looking for stories among the minnows. They found Haas and, thanks partly to Steiner's candid cursing, the series and Steiner became a huge hit.

STEWARDS

Race weekends have four stewards selected from a panel of FIA-qualified officials who make decisions across a race weekend. They can give judgements and hand out penalties using the regulations agreed on by all teams. There is usually a former F1 driver and a local steward who has specific knowledge of the track.

SIR JACKIE STEWART

Nicknamed the 'Flying Scot', Sir John Young Stewart OBE was born in Scotland, and would become a three-time World Champion and tireless safety advocate for F1. He is dyslexic but wasn't diagnosed until the 1980s, so didn't excel at school, being called stupid by his teachers and fellow students. It didn't stop Sir Jackie from becoming one of the most successful drivers of all time.

He raced with other legends such as Graham Hill, Jim Clark and Emerson Fittipaldi. Stewart saw many of his fellow drivers killed at racetracks, and in 1966, at Spa-Francorchamps, he had his own brush with death, driving off the track in the pouring rain at 266kph. He crashed into a telegraph pole and a shed before coming to rest in a farmer's building, his leg pinned by his steering column, and the fuel tank spilling onto Stewart. He was rescued by Hill and Bob Bondurant, who had also crashed nearby. Stewart survived but that, and the later death of his teammate François Cevert, made him a staunch advocate for better safety in Formula One, which hasn't always been received well. 'I would have been a much more popular World Champion if I had always said what people wanted to hear. I might have been dead, but definitely more popular.'

Sir Jackie can often be found guiding groups of F1 guests through the paddock and is never short of a story, even well into his eighties! I still remember the day Lewis Hamilton won his third World Championship, to draw level with Stewart's achievement. As Hamilton celebrated in the paddock after the race, Sir Jackie found Lewis and gave him a massive man-hug, as if passing the baton of success over to the Englishman.

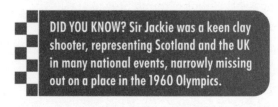
DID YOU KNOW? Sir Jackie was a keen clay shooter, representing Scotland and the UK in many national events, narrowly missing out on a place in the 1960 Olympics.

STRATEGY

You might think that driving flat out and being the fastest driver is the best way to win a race. However, there are many more things for a driver to consider if he wants to win a race, and strategy is one of the key elements.

In Grand Prix racing (in the dry) every driver must stop at least once to change their tyres. There are three types of tyre for a race: soft, medium and hard. These each wear down at a different rate – soft usually wear down the fastest but they give the most grip, whereas a hard tyre will last longer but not be as quick.

Using vast amounts of data and research, the strategy team will look at key factors for a specific race. For example, how long will it take to drive in and out of the pits? What are the chances of a safety car? This will give a base-line strategy.

Before every race Pirelli (official tyre suppliers to F1) issue a strategy guide that shows if a team start on a certain tyre, how many laps they are likely to be able to complete before coming into the pits to change tyres. This can change depending on whether a driver is having to attack or defend or if they are driving in clear air, with less stress and wear on the tyres.

If you're trying to overtake a rival and can't pass them on track, you can use strategy to try and pass them:

> » **The Undercut:** You pit earlier than your rival and have fresher tyres to use aggressively. They will be on older tyres until they pit, meaning they will be slower.

This is the preferred method, as the new tyres give an advantage without necessarily needing a car to be faster in pace.

» **The Overcut:** This is when you stay out later than the car you are trying to get past, hoping to build up a big enough lead to come out ahead after you've pitted.

A planned strategy can go up in smoke easily and quickly – e.g., due to mechanical issues, a rain shower or a safety car – and a strategist will have many different scenarios worked out to deal with every situation.

One of the key factors to calling a good strategy is predicting where a gap will be, how those gaps are changing throughout the course of the race, and how you can give your car 'free air'. The last thing you want to do is bring your driver into the pits and release them right into a battle, you need to try and give them the time and space to warm their tyres up, not have to fight straight away.

And, of course, you always have to be ready to react when you see what strategy your rivals are adopting. All the strategists I have had the pleasure of meeting and chatting to are highly educated, with a keen interest in maths and science. It is pretty hard to outsmart them. My tip is never to play drinking games with a strategist – you will lose!

LANCE STROLL

Lance Stroll (actual name Strulovitch) was born on 29 October 1998 in Montreal, Canada, to parents Claire-

Anne Callens and Lawrence Stroll, a Canadian businessman currently worth a reported $3.9bn.

Stroll started karting aged ten and won rookie of the year in 2009; he was signed the following year for the Ferrari Driver Academy. Stroll was crowned 2014 Italian F4 Champion driving for the Prema team, which his father bought a stake in, and Stroll went on to race in the F3 European Championship alongside Charles Leclerc, George Russell and Alex Albon.

Williams came calling and Stroll left the FDA to become test driver for the Oxfordshire-based team alongside Felipe Massa, his father heavily investing in the team as he supported his son on their shared mission – to succeed in F1.

In 2017, at the Azerbaijan GP, Stroll finished third, becoming the youngest rookie to get a podium. I remember being immensely impressed in Monza that year as Stroll wrestled with the rain in qualifying to set an incredible lap, the fourth fastest. Thanks to grid penalties for the two Red Bulls, he started the Italian GP in second place, making him the youngest F1 driver to start a race from the front row at 18 years and 310 days.

Stroll moved to Racing Point in 2019 after his father bought the team and changed the name to Aston Martin. He has stayed there ever since, with the team bringing in Sebastian Vettel and Fernando Alonso as Stroll's teammates. Stroll Sr has invested heavily in the team and both he and his son hope success will come.

T is for

TEAR-OFF STRIP, TELEMETRY, TIMING, JEAN TODT, YUKI TSUNODA and TYRES

TEAR-OFF STRIP

These are the see-through plastic strips that a driver fits to their helmet's visor before the start of the race. It means they can tear off a strip that might have dirt or rain affecting their vision. Drivers have up to five tear-offs, ready to be ripped off from either side, whichever the driver prefers. Beware though, it's not unheard of for tear-off strips to cause serious damage to a following car, as they can get sucked into the radiator or brake ducts and end a race for anyone unlucky enough for this fate to befall them.

TELEMETRY

Telemetry is the science of measuring, recording and transmitting a vehicle's motion data. In Formula One, telemetry is gathered in real-time and beamed wirelessly from the car to the engineering team. It provides a huge amount of detailed feedback about every aspect of the driver's and car's performance, from driving style and speed to the exact settings of the car.

TIMING

F1 has come a long way with timing. It used to be a role carried out by the wives and girlfriends of drivers in the old days. They would sit with a stopwatch and a clipboard and time each lap. Nowadays, timing is state-of-the-art, with GPS transponders fitted to each car, and timing beams on every racetrack. Not as charming, but definitely more efficient.

JEAN TODT

Jean Todt is an essential part of the story of Formula One and the sport it is today. He and Bernie Ecclestone were, in essence, the founding fathers of modern F1. After a long career as a rally co-driver, Todt became director of Peugeot Talbot Sport. In 1994 he moved into F1 with Ferrari, overseeing their rejuvenation to become the dominant team on the grid for several years. From 2009 he served three terms as president of the FIA at a time of huge change for the sport, stepping down at the end of 2021.

Todt is now the United Nations Special Envoy for Road Safety and is passionate about making driving safer globally. Married to actress Michelle Yeoh, Todt has one son by a previous marriage, Nicolas Todt, who is a successful motorsport manager, representing the likes of Charles Leclerc and Felipe Massa.

YUKI TSUNODA

Tsunoda carries on the proud tradition of Japanese Formula One drivers, becoming the 18th from that country. He joined the Honda Formula Dream Project from 2016 and then Red Bull from 2019 when Honda began working with them. Tsunoda has been managed heavily by the Red Bull Junior Team, even moving to their Faenza base in Italy to get into shape.

Tsunoda got his chance to drive in F1 in 2021, for Alpha Tauri, being mentored by Alex Albon and partnering Pierre

Gasly until 2022. Gasly, far more experienced than his new teammate, acted almost as an older brother to Tsunoda, until he moved to Alpine for the 2023 season and Tsunoda found himself leading the team.

Tsunoda's personality is well documented thanks to a whole episode of *Drive to Survive* which followed his journey; his fondness for food, his messy room and his love of gaming and sleeping had young fans falling for Yuki all over the world.

TYRES

They are black and round: you might not think there's anything more to know about tyres. The ones fitted to your own car might even be Pirelli tyres, just like on an F1 car. However, the differences are key. Pirelli make 18-inch (457mm) tyres for F1 cars that are not made to last. Unlike your tyres, they are designed to degrade to try to make the racing more exciting.

Tyres come in two types in F1 – dry or 'slick' tyres, and wet tyres (which include 'intermediate' tyres). There are five slick tyres for Pirelli to choose from and two wet-weather tyres.

If we look at the slicks first, they range from the C1, C2, C3, C4 and C5. The C1 is the hardest and C5 the softest. Each weekend Pirelli nominate three tyres from their range – with drivers getting eight sets of the soft (red-banded) tyres, three mediums (yellow), and two hard (white) sets to last throughout the weekend.

Each team will also have wet-weather tyres in case it rains. These are the intermediate tyre (green-banded) and the full-wet tyre (blue-banded). The intermediate is used when it's wet, but no standing water is on the track; it has grooves cut into it and is the tyre that most resembles a road tyre. The full wet is used in heavy rain. Judging when and whether to use full wets and intermediates is crucial in F1. If you switch to a tyre when the conditions aren't quite right, you may end up losing a lot of time or even crashing out.

Tyres like to be warm and have special blankets which they are wrapped and stored in. These blankets are heated to 70°C. If a session is delayed in the rain and it's a cold day, you can often find drivers warming themselves up by hugging the tyre blankets!

DID YOU KNOW? At 300kph, a single intermediate tyre can disperse around 35 to 40 litres of water per second. That means that a Formula One car at full speed on the straight can shift around 150 litres of water per second. If it's on the full wet, that figure can be doubled.

U is for UNITED STATES and UNSAFE RELEASE

UNITED STATES

The US has become a massive market for F1 since *Drive to Survive* came along. Bernie Ecclestone always wanted to 'crack America' and brought F1 to Las Vegas in the early 1980s, but it didn't take off until he left the sport and new US owners Liberty Media bought F1 in 2017.

Twelve different venues have hosted F1 races:

- Sebring, Florida
- Riverside, California
- Watkins Glen, New York
- Long Beach, California
- Dallas Fair Park, Texas
- Detroit, Michigan
- Phoenix, Arizona
- Indianapolis, Indiana
- Caesars Palace, Las Vegas, Nevada
- Circuit of the Americas, Austin, Texas
- Miami, Florida
- Las Vegas Strip, Nevada

Austin, Miami and Las Vegas are currently venues for F1 races in the US, making the States the country with the most F1 races each year. Every team is very aware of the growth of the sport in America, with RB and Williams hosting their car launches in the US ahead of the 2024 season.

F1 is a global brand worth billions of dollars, and with Lewis Hamilton's move to Ferrari, it's hard to see this trend doing anything but going upwards. I love going to the States for F1. The vibe is quite different from other countries we visit. Fans embrace the whole weekend, not just the race. They really buy into the sport.

UNSAFE RELEASE

This is when a car leaves their pit box in a manner that endangers either personnel or other drivers in the pit lane (normally because another car is about to head past them at the time), for example causing another car to crash, slow excessively or run over equipment or people. I've seen all of these happen and it's usually caused by miscommunication between the driver and the pit crew.

V is for
MAX VERSTAPPEN
and SEBASTIAN VETTEL

How to Read F1

MAX VERSTAPPEN

Max is one of the greatest drivers of our era, and maybe of all time (he's still writing his name into the record books). He became the youngest ever F1 driver when he fulfilled his destiny by signing with Red Bull to drive for the Toro Rosso team at just 17 years and 166 days.

The son of international karter Sophie Kumpen and F1 driver Jos Verstappen, racing was always in his blood. His parents split up when he was young, and not long after he started living with his dad in the Netherlands. The two of them toured Europe, dominating the karting scene, sharing the ambition of Max becoming an F1 champion.

Verstappen didn't hang about in the junior categories: after just one season racing single-seaters in Formula 3 in 2014, aged just 16 (winning a record six consecutive races, ten victories in total), he made the move to F1 with the Red Bull Junior Team. Mercedes were interested in signing him too, with Toto Wolff meeting with Max and Jos, but they were only able to offer him a Formula 2 seat (Hamilton and Rosberg were the Mercedes drivers at the time). The promise of a race seat at Toro Rosso saw Verstappen sign with Red Bull. If you chat to Wolff, he admits he regrets not signing Max when he had the chance.

I remember when Max began his F1 career, the paddock was awash with people saying he was too young. Mika Häkkinen told the BBC, 'In F1 you don't go to learn, you have to be ready.' But Verstappen did his talking on track, scoring points in only his second ever F1 race and picking up Rookie of the Year for the 2015 season.

After only 14 months in Formula One, Verstappen was promoted to the Red Bull team, winning his debut race for the team, the Spanish Grand Prix of 2016, becoming the youngest driver ever to win an F1 race.

Verstappen has a natural talent for racing: his feeling in the car, his mental capacity, his total dedication and commitment are all outstanding. He impressed everyone with his sublime performances, but he was fast becoming a controversial figure, with his aggressive on-track action often ending with a crash. For a time, Verstappen showed his immaturity in handling difficult situations off track. Once, when he was asked repeatedly about crashing in every one of the first six races of the 2018 season, he snapped back, 'I get tired of the questions. If I get a few more, I might headbutt someone.' However, as Verstappen has grown with the sport, he has matured and now is a very different person, controlling that wild side off track, and almost faultless on track.

When I interviewed Max at the end of the 2019 season for BBC Radio 5 Live, I asked him if he thought he could be a World Champion in the future. With steely determination, he looked at me directly in the eyes and said, 'Given the right car, of course I can be a World Champion. I just need the right car.'

He didn't have to wait too long. Red Bull and Adrian Newey developed the RB16B for the 2021 season. Verstappen won his first title, but it was a season riddled with controversy as Lewis Hamilton and Max Verstappen traded clashes on track, and Toto Wolff and Christian Horner duked it out (metaphorically) off track. It would be one of the most controversial and bitter endings to an F1 World Championship in the history of the sport.

The popularity of F1 reached an all-time high, though, with everyone talking about the moment Verstappen won his first world title, and whether Hamilton was robbed of his record-breaking eighth. It split the fans and, in 2022, partisan crowds filed onto F1 tracks, booing their anti-hero. Verstappen took it all in his stride, and with a sea of orange fans (the Dutch) following him around the world, he won his second title in impressive style, winning 15 races. In 2023, Verstappen completed the most dominant season in F1 history, winning his third consecutive World Championship with a record 19 wins from 22 races.

Whether you love Max or not, you have to appreciate what he can do with an F1 car. He is sublime. In fact, he is so talented he makes it look easy. He is in perfect union with his car and, together with Red Bull, we have now definitely entered the Verstappen era. What he can achieve is unknown at this point – maybe he will go on to break all the records – but one thing is for sure, in every sense of the word Verstappen was *born* to be an F1 World Champion.

DID YOU KNOW? Max likes driving so much that when he's not in an F1 car, you can often find him sim racing. He has even had a simulator installed in his motorhome for the European F1 races, so when he finishes at the track he can come back and practise/play some more. He's part of Redline Racing team and believes sim racing is an integral part of his training regime.

SEBASTIAN VETTEL

One of the most successful drivers in Formula One history, Sebastian Vettel is a four-time World Champion, a father of three and a keen activist. He dominated the sport from 2010 until 2013 with Red Bull, winning 53 races in his career.

Born in Heppenheim, West Germany, on 3 July 1987, to parents Norbert and Heike, Vettel grew up watching Michael Schumacher dominating F1. The front and back pages of the newspapers were covered in photos of the great 'Schumi'.

Vettel got his first kart at three but had to wait until he was eight before he could start racing. He won the 2004 Formula BMW ADAC Championship, winning 18 of the 20 races. It put him on the radar of F1 teams and he was invited to test for Williams and Sauber.

His F1 debut was for Sauber at the 2007 US Grand Prix in Indianapolis, where he scored points, finishing eighth. He was released by BMW Sauber in July of that year to take up a place with Red Bull's Toro Rosso team. In a rare comment to media, Red Bull owner Dietrich Mateschitz tipped Vettel to become a big star in F1, saying he had 'extraordinary potential'.

Vettel's first win came in impressive style, at a wet Monza in the 2008 Italian Grand Prix; he led most of the race and ended up finishing 12.5 seconds ahead of the field. The German media lapped up this exciting new talent, giving him the name 'Baby Schumi'.

He was promoted to Red Bull in 2009 when David Coulthard retired, and in the third race of the season won his first race for the team at the Chinese Grand Prix – it was Red Bull's first ever win. Vettel's teammate was Mark Webber, and the pair had a difficult relationship, leading to collisions and clashes on and off track. However, Red Bull were an exciting new outfit with great talent behind the wheel, and soon Vettel and the team won their first world title.

In 2010–13, Sebastian Vettel and Red Bull dominated Formula One, with pole positions aplenty, and often Vettel would lead every lap of the race without being challenged. It was an outstanding partnership.

Sebastian Vettel

The rule change in 2014 saw him struggle to win a race, however, and in Japan later that year Vettel surprised us all by announcing he would leave Red Bull to join a team he had always loved, Ferrari. Christian Horner was visibly shocked when he spoke to us that morning. Vettel had only given his boss and friend a few hours' notice before making his statement public and ending his contract with the team a year early.

Vettel challenged for a fifth title with Ferrari, but it wasn't to be, and after five seasons with the Scuderia his contract was not renewed. He joined Aston Martin for a couple of years, becoming a mentor to Lance Stroll, but Vettel would never return to winning ways and he announced his retirement from F1 in July 2022, hanging up his race helmet at the end of the year.

As a director of the Grand Prix Drivers' Association, Vettel was a hugely respected driver and stood alongside Lewis Hamilton when campaigning for Black Lives Matter. He also appeared on the BBC's *Question Time* to discuss the climate crisis and Brexit. During the 2021 British GP, he went into the grandstands at Silverstone to join volunteers and fans picking up litter. He lives in Switzerland with his wife, Hanna Prater, and likes to live life out of the spotlight, just like his childhood hero, Michael Schumacher.

DID YOU KNOW? Vettel always named his cars in F1, starting with Julie in 2008. His first title came with Luscious Liz and Randy Mandy, and he also had Kinky Kylie and Hungry Heidi … to name just a few.

W is for WILLIAMS, SUSIE WOLFF, TOTO WOLFF, WOMEN and WORLD CHAMPIONS

WILLIAMS

One of the most prestigious teams in F1, Sir Frank Williams set up his team in Didcot in 1977 (moving to their current Grove location in 1996), along with his good friend Sir Patrick Head. It took the team just two years to get their first win, with Clay Regazzoni winning the British GP at Silverstone in 1979. The momentum behind Williams F1 continued to grow and they took their first piece of silverware the following year, picking up the Constructors' Championship, with Alan Jones taking the drivers' title. It was a magnificent achievement for Sir Frank and his team.

Williams F1 have won nine constructors' and seven drivers' titles since their inception in 1977, making them the second most successful team of all time (behind Ferrari). Some of the biggest names in F1 have driven for Williams, including Keke Rosberg, Nigel Mansell, Damon Hill, David Coulthard, Jenson Button, Jacques Villeneuve and Ayrton Senna.

It wasn't always like that, though. Early in his career, Sir Frank and his wife Ginny travelled the racetracks of the world, hauling sometimes decrepit cars from country to country. They had little money and a friend lent them the £8 it cost to buy a licence to get married. Determination and a competitive drive saw Sir Frank graduate from amateur racing all the way to the most elite levels of motorsport. He was gifted, had no time for losing, and lived life to the absolute max.

However, tragedy struck when Sir Frank was involved in a car crash in 1986. Williams had been at a test at Paul

Ricard but was keen to make it home in time for the London half-marathon that he was due to race the following day. Speeding to the airport, the hire car crashed and rolled, leaving Sir Frank fighting for his life. The accident caused him to lose the use of all four of his limbs, becoming a tetraplegic – but nothing would stop him from returning to the sport he loved. He was a man devoted to winning, and stubborn with it.

I spent some of my favourite times in the paddock with Sir Frank. Like many of the men in F1 – even confined to his wheelchair and with a carer by his side almost 24/7 – he had that familiar glint in his eye, and he was full of mischief. He went on to be the oldest tetraplegic in the world before his death in 2021, aged 79.

There wasn't a single person in the paddock who didn't have a special memory of Sir Frank. He was such a personality within F1. Lewis Hamilton said of him, 'Sir Frank Williams was one of the kindest people I had the pleasure of meeting in this sport. What he achieved is something truly special. Until his last days I know he remained a racer and a fighter at heart. His legacy will live on forever.'

For many, the romance of Williams – a privateer team going up against the biggest automotive brands in the world and beating them – is the reason they fell in love with F1. The famous blue, yellow and white livery was so synonymous with winning through the 1980s and 90s. I remember the scenes of Nigel Mansell being mobbed by fans at Silverstone in 1992 as they celebrated his win at the British Grand Prix, his Williams swamped as 'Mansell Mania' took over.

After Sir Frank stepped down as team principal, his daughter Claire took over, only the second female to be a team principal. But with financial pressures taking their toll on the team, investment was needed and new owners, a consortium called Dorilton Capital, took over. Former Mercedes man James Vowles is now team principal and has set about remodelling the team to be more competitive in the future.

SUSIE WOLFF

Born in Oban, Scotland, in 1982, Susie Wolff (née Stoddart) is one of the most influential figures in motorsport. Married to Toto (with a son, Jack), the pair are the ultimate powerhouse couple.

Her parents own a motorcycle dealership in her hometown and her father John raced motorbikes in his younger days. In fact, Wolff's mum and dad first met when her mum bought her first motorbike from her dad's shop. Wolff started karting aged eight, before graduating to Formula Renault and Formula 3. A move to DTM racing in Germany followed, where she raced in 2006–12 with Mücke Motorsport.

She became development driver for the Williams F1 team in April 2012 and took part in two practice sessions during the British and German Grand Prix weekends, becoming the first woman to take part in an F1 race weekend in over 20 years.

Realising she had reached as far as she could go in F1, at the end of 2015 Wolff announced her retirement on the BBC, expressing her intent to help other women in motorsport.

She founded the 'Dare to Be Different' initiative to raise awareness of opportunities for girls in motorsport.

In 2018, Wolff was appointed team principal for the Venturi Formula E team, where she would rise to become CEO. But her greatest success to many has been launching the F1 Academy, a new all-female racing series designed to run alongside F1 weekends, with female drivers affiliated to F1 teams. As managing director, Wolff has taken it upon herself to make sure there is a route into motorsport for female drivers, not just males, saying, 'I knew I wanted to give something back when I stopped racing. I never set out to become a role model but somehow I did. The opportunities are out there.'

TOTO WOLFF

Torger Christian 'Toto' Wolff is an Austrian billionaire who use to race cars, and now at the helm of Mercedes, is one of the most successful team principals in F1. Born in Vienna in 1972, he was only eight when his father was diagnosed with a brain tumour. It changed everything, as Wolff found himself looking after his sister and mother. Their affluent lifestyle had to be given up and the family moved to a small apartment. Speaking on the BBC's *Desert Island Discs* in 2023, he said, 'You don't wish [on] any child or adolescent such a situation. But it has shaped me in a way that my determination is strong, and my resilience levels are high. You know, when we don't perform in Formula One, that doesn't even move the needle. For me, that is so far away from suffering or pain.'

How to Read F1

 **DID YOU KNOW?** When travelling the world with F1, Toto Wolff eats the same thing every day ... He starts with pumpernickel bread with butter and some ham, then a small cappuccino – so he can have another half an hour later – and then it's chicken breast with tomato salad. And he has the same for dinner.

His father died when Toto was 15 years old. Clearly driven to succeed, Wolff set up a series of successful investment companies. To say he fell into motorsport is not far from the truth. He tells of a time when he was first invited to an F3 race and walked on the track when the grid was lining up. He felt a massive explosion within him. He found it fascinating.

In 1992, Wolff began dabbling in motorsport, driving in Austrian and German Formula Ford races, before winning the 24 Hours Nürburgring in 1994. Dabbling turned into a passion and in 2009, after spells in GT racing and rallying, Wolff bought a share in the Williams F1 team and joined the board, later becoming executive director. He also set up his own driver management company alongside former F1 driver Mika Häkkinen, shaping the careers of many drivers including Valtteri Bottas and Esteban Ocon.

Mercedes appointed Wolff as executive director in 2013, making him team principal. Wolff now owns a 33 per cent stake of the F1 team. During his time at Mercedes, with Niki Lauda by his side, Wolff successfully led them to a record eight consecutive constructors' titles (2014–21), managed the fractious 2016 title battle between Rosberg and Hamilton, and is now handling the departure of the most successful driver of all time, as Lewis Hamilton leaves the team for Ferrari in 2025.

WOMEN

Five female drivers have entered a Grand Prix since the Formula One Championship began in 1950.

- » **Maria Teresa de Filippis** was the first woman to qualify for an F1 race. She had five entries and started three grands prix in 1958–9, racing for Maserati and Behra-Porsche. Her best result was tenth in the 1958 Belgian Grand Prix in Spa (a points-paying position if the rules had been as they are today.) It would be 15 years before another female broke into F1.

- » **Lella Lombardi** had 17 entries and 12 starts, scoring half a point at the 1975 Spanish Grand Prix, making her the most successful female F1 driver of all time. The Italian raced for March, RAM and Williams in the 1970s.

- » **Divina Galica** drove for Surtees and Hesketh in 1976 and 1978 but failed to qualify for a Grand Prix. She was an accomplished skier, representing Britain in four Winter Olympics before transferring her speed onto the track. She is one of seven drivers to represent their country in an Olympics.

» **Desiré Wilson**, from South Africa, drove a Williams once in 1980 but failed to qualify. However, she became the only woman to win a Formula One race of any kind when she won at Brands Hatch in the British Aurora F1 Championship. She went on to compete in CART in the US and tried to qualify for the Indy 500. Wilson is widely recognised as one of the most accomplished female racing drivers ever.

» The last female to compete in F1 was Italian **Giovanna Amati**, who drove for Brabham in 1992. She entered three races but failed to qualify.

Susie Wolff took part in an F1 race weekend, driving in the first practice session of the British Grand Prix in 2014. It was 22 years after the last female driver took to a track in an official F1 session.

Test and development programmes are acting as an important way of bringing more females more visibility, with two-time W Series champion Jamie Chadwick signing with Williams, and Jess Hawkins with Aston Martin, but it still feels like we are some way from another female taking part in a Formula One race. With championships like W Series and the F1 Academy set up to make the path to F1 more accessible for female drivers, the future looks brighter, but right now the F1 grid comprises 20 men and no women.

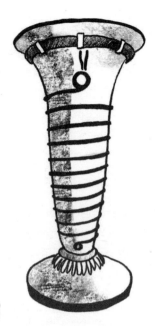

WORLD CHAMPIONS

Seventy-three F1 world titles have been contested (correct as of 2023); 34 different drivers have won them, from 15 different countries.

- » The first World Champion was Italian Giuseppe Farina for Alfa Romeo in 1950.
- » Max Verstappen is the current champion.
- » Michael Schumacher holds the record for the most consecutive titles with five (2000–4).
- » Juan Manuel Fangio was the oldest World Champion at 46 years old.
- » The UK has the most F1 drivers' titles, with 10 drivers winning 20 titles between them.

F1 World Championship Wins

Drivers	Number of titles won
Michael Schumacher and Lewis Hamilton	7
Juan Manuel Fangio	5
Alain Prost and Sebastian Vettel	4
Jack Brabham, Jackie Stewart, Niki Lauda, Nelson Piquet, Ayrton Senna and Max Verstappen (Verstappen will probably have four by the end of 2024)	3
Alberto Ascari, Graham Hill, Jim Clark, Emerson Fittipaldi, Mika Häkkinen and Fernando Alonso	2
Giuseppe Farina, Mike Hawthorn, Phil Hill, John Surtees, Denny Hulme, Jochen Rindt, James Hunt, Mario Andretti, Jody Scheckter, Alan Jones, Keke Rosberg, Nigel Mansell, Damon Hill, Jacques Villeneuve, Kimi Räikkönen, Jenson Button and Nico Rosberg	1

X is for

X-WING

X-WING

In 1997, Tyrrell tried a new concept to add downforce to their car, the X-Wing. The team had found a loophole in the regulations, allowing Tyrrell to place winglets high and wide of the car's main body to capture airflow in the freestream.

It was claimed the X-wing contributed around 5 per cent of the car's total downforce. It triggered an intense but short development war, before the FIA intervened and banned X-wings, arguing that they created an uneven playing field, as teams with more resources and technology were better able to design and implement more advanced X-wings.

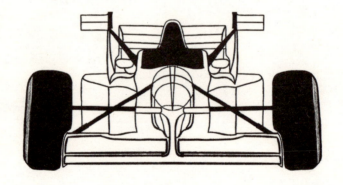

Y is for YACHTS

How to Read F1

YACHTS

Yachts have been an integral part of the Monaco Grand Prix weekend since the race began in 1929. Owners and their guests got a front-row seat as the cars sped along the waterfront. As F1 has grown, so too have the yachts. Classic sailing yachts lined the harbour in the 1950s when the first F1 Championship race took place (won by Fangio in the Alfa Romeo). By the 1970s the cars looked a lot more modern, as did the yachts, which were now powered by motor.

The 1980s were all about power-dressing and the start of the testosterone-heavy show of 'mine is bigger than yours!' Yachts were moved closer to the action, lining the harbour wall, providing the perfect place to have a party (wearing as little as possible), while Alain Prost mastered Monaco in his McLaren.

The early 2000s brought along super-yachts and tighter security, as organisers built crash fences to separate yachts from the on-track action and all boats harbourside had to move off from the seawall when sessions were on track (just in case someone crashed).

DID YOU KNOW? Lawrence Stroll's yacht was one of the biggest at the Monaco GP in 2023. Called *Faith*, she's 97m long, has nine cabins, annual running costs of $15–20m and cost $200m. *Faith* was recently bought by fellow Canadian billionaire Michael Latifi, father of former F1 driver Nicholas Latifi.

Yachts

As the appeal of F1 has grown, so too have the yachts, with Port Hercules transformed for the week into a luxurious backdrop for hosting VIPs and celebrities. Why book a hotel room when you can stay on a super-yacht for the race? If you fancy chartering a yacht for the race, make sure you pack your wallet because packages start from £60,000, and that's just for a tiddler!

Size does matter when it comes to yachts: if you're too big to berth inside the harbour, you have to watch the race from afar. Only yachts under 135m long can fit into Port Hercules. During the race weekend Monaco manages to squeeze 700 yachts into the harbour, ranging from the small classic sailing yachts all the way up to the megabucks super-yachts. I've been lucky enough to slip off my shoes and try out a couple of the bigger ocean-farers in my time, and they are as good as they look, with a level of luxury that's out of this world.

Other circuits have tried to emulate Monaco, with the Yas Marina having its own 'mini-Monaco'-style harbour that the racing wraps around. The HMS *Murray Walker* always takes up residency in the corner closest to the paddock, but it doesn't have exactly the same appeal as Monte Carlo in May.

How to Read F1

So, what happens when you want to 'wow' but have no water? No problem. When Miami came to the party in 2022, they just built a fake marina. Have your super-yacht craned into Bayfront Park and just pretend the cool sea-breeze is washing over you.

Z is for
ZHOU GUANYU

ZHOU GUANYU

Zhou is the first Chinese driver in F1 history. He started karting at eight and made the move to the UK in 2012, basing himself in Sheffield, where he drove for the Strawberry Racing team. Success in the junior categories put him on the radar of F1 teams; he joined Ferrari's driver academy, followed by Renault. He completed his first F1 practice session at the Austrian GP in 2021 and joined Alfa Romeo in 2022, but with a relatively uncompetitive car, Zhou has only been able to record a best finish of eighth in the Canadian GP in 2022.

The biggest moment in his career finally came in 2024 when Zhou raced in front of his home fans as the Chinese Grand Prix returned to the calendar for the first time since Covid. It was a long-held dream for the little boy who was born in Shanghai in 1999, not far from where the race is held. He said, 'I'm so proud of where I'm from – the support I've received from everyone back home. I race for them. I want to show that, even though we aren't known for motorsports, we can still be great. That we can be *fast*. That we are a racing nation.'

DID YOU KNOW? Zhou drives the number 24 car in honour of his sporting hero Kobe Bryant, who famously wore the number 24 shirt for the LA Lakers.

REFERENCES

Rosberg, Keke, cited by Paul Weaver in '"Nico Knows What It Means to Me," Says Keke after Rosberg Family F1 Double', theguardian.com (2016)

Vettel, Sebastian, 'F1 2016 Canadian GP', Fans of Sebastian Vettel (2016)

Gasly, Pierre, cited by Valentin Khorounzhiy in 'Pierre Gasly's anguish at loss of "best mate" Anthoine Hubert', autosport.com (2019)

Brundle, Martin, cited by Alex Kirshner in 'F1 Commentator Martin Brundle on inventing the grid walk, driving legendary cars, and why the sport should always be a little scary,' gq-magazine.co.uk (2022)

Hamilton, Lewis, BBC Radio 5 Live (2013)

Hamilton, Lewis, cited by Jonathan Noble in 'World champion Lewis Hamilton interview', autosport.com (2008)

Hamilton, Lewis, cited by James Galloway in 'Lewis Hamilton officially crowned 2014 world champion in award-laden weekend', skysports.com (2014)

Lauda, Niki, cited by Gerald Donaldson in 'Hall of Fame: James Hunt', formula1.com

Watson, John, cited in 'Mclaren MP4-1', f1technical.net

The Lauda family, cited in 'Three time F1 world champion Niki Lauda passes away', formula1.com (2019)

Verstappen, Max, cited in 'Verstappen: No such thing as a low risk lap in Monaco', grandprix247.com (2017)

Newey, Adrian, cited by Donald McRae in 'Ayrton Senna's death "changed me physically", says Adrian Newey', theguardian.com (2011)

Prost, Alain, cited by Gerald Donaldson in 'Hall of Fame: Alain Prost', formula1.com

Prost, Alain, 'Alain Prost on Ayrton Senna: "Between us, we can screw all the others!"', autoweek.com (2014)

Ricciardo, Daniel, 'Not Done With F1', *F1 Beyond the Grid* podcast (2022)

Wolff, Toto, cited by Jon Wilde in 'Wolff was charmed by Russell's PowerPoint plan', planetf1.com (2021)

Anderson, Gary, speaking to the author in Belgium (2013)

Donaldson, Gerald, *Grand Prix People: Revelations from Inside the Formula 1 Circus*, Motor Racing Publications Ltd (1990)

Stewart, Jackie, cited by John Brooks in 'Retrospective: Grand Prix and The Man Part 4', speedhunters.com (2009)

Verstappen, Max, cited by Andrew Benson in 'Max Verstappen: Red Bull driver says he "might headbutt someone"', bbc.co.uk/sport (2018)

Mateschitz, Dietrich, cited in 'Vettel could be a star', skysports.com (2008)

Hamilton, Lewis, cited in 'Lewis Hamilton on Frank Williams', silverarrows.net (2021)

Wolff, Susie, cited by Andrew Benson in 'Susie Wolff to launch initiative for women in motorsport', bbc.co.uk/sport (2016)

Gyuanu, Zhou, 'I Want You To Know This About Me', The Players' Tribune (2023)

ACKNOWLEDGEMENTS

Writing a book when you're recovering from a stroke is no mean feat so there are a million people I would like to thank. Firstly, my family who have moved heaven and earth to offer their love and support – both the Gows (especially my mum, dad and brother), and the Coleys (especially Caroline, Stephen, Matt and Kate) – and to my wonderful husband Jamie, and daughter Izzy.

To my closest friends who have supported me through this process, including my mum chums Annie, Jenna and Soozie, and to Louise, Kate, Ben, Vicky, Ali and Susi.

To all at my publishers Penguin Random House, especially Nell Warner who first convinced me that writing a book was a good idea, and latterly Katie Fisher, whose tireless work and support has been unwavering. To designer Jack Smyth for bringing his own unique and award-winning style to the illustrations in this book and its cover. Also to copyeditor Ian Allen for his time and effort as he painstakingly worked to correct my dyslexic words (a condition brought on by my stroke).

To my producers (and friends) Jason Swales, Chessie Bent, Patrick Whiteside and Joe Aldridge and everyone at the BBC and IMG (who produce the BBC's F1 output). Special shoutouts to the 'bosses': Ben Gallop and Richard Maddock (BBC), Ollie Kneen and Steve Tebb (IMG). Having spent so many years travelling the world with F1, I must give a special mention to Jack and Jolyon too, who looked out for me and made the sometimes gruelling schedule far more enjoyable.

To the world of F1, where to begin ... To the awe-inspiring F1 drivers, without your bravery and unwavering commitment to the sport, I wouldn't have one of the best jobs in the world. To all the fans who have inspired this book, thank you! There are so many amazing people who have offered their words of wisdom and support in this wonderful (and slightly crazy) world we live and work in. Firstly, to David Tremayne who made me believe. My great thanks to Ben Edwards for taking the time to read this book and help pick up some of the mistakes I made. Also, to Damon Hill, Nico Rosberg and Valtteri Bottas for their words of support. To Ben Hunt, Gerald Donaldson, Bec Clancy, Will Buxton, Maurice Hamilton, Gary Anderson, Garry Connelly, Marc Priestly, Craig Scarborough and Sam Collins. To all the F1 team PRs and bosses who have supported this project, all at F1 headquarters and the great folks at *Drive to Survive*, Netflix and Box to Box, especially Tom Rogers and Paul Martin.

And to the many others who have offered me support, advice, and help along the way. I'm 100 per cent sure I've forgotten someone important, so please accept my apologies.

Finally, to all the amazing therapists I've been treated by, especially my speech and language team who have spent many hours helping me: Emma, Tammy, Nicola, Natalie, Lisa, Sahin, Lisa Harris and all at the Stroke Association and Different Strokes.

This book is dedicated to all those who have had a stroke or are still struggling with stroke recovery. Never in my wildest dreams would I have believed that I would be able to write a book after my stroke, but with love, support and fierce dedication (hours of therapy 'homework' to make my brain learn how to form words, write and type again) here I am, a published author. Believe …

ABOUT THE AUTHOR

Broadcaster and presenter, mum and wife, Jennie Gow broke into the world of Formula One motor racing in 2011 and has since become renowned as one of the sport's foremost media professionals.

One of the few women to work in this demanding arena, Jennie is currently to be found presenting and reporting on the BBC's award-winning Formula One coverage. She also features as an F1 expert on the hit Netflix documentary series *Drive to Survive*. Most recently, she has taken on the ground-breaking role of co-lead commentator of the Extreme E racing series, championing diversity.

Setting an incredible example for the cause of Women in Sport, Jennie has mentored girls and young women eager to learn from her success. This has included being an ambassador for the FIA Girls on Track programme and creating her own webinar series to encourage people from all backgrounds into the world of motorsport media.

Jennie has presented many documentaries, a passion of hers since her first job at the BBC. She was nominated for the SJA's 'Best Radio Documentary of the Year' in 2015 for her work on the BBC's James Hunt special, and in 2017 Jennie co-produced the BBC 5 Live 'grid girl's debate' documentary which started the conversation on the subject.

Away from motor-powered action, Jennie is a knowledgeable and respected sports presenter and reporter, having honed her skills on Sky Sports News for several years. She has also presented World Cup Rowing, T20 World Cup Cricket, the

Women's FA Cup Final and is a regular pundit (and show winner) on BBC Radio 5 Live's *Fighting Talk*.

Jennie married her husband, Jamie, in 2012 and they now share their love of F1 by both working in the fast-paced and thrilling sport. Their family grew in 2016 with the arrival of their daughter, Izzy. Jennie dreams of one day taking part in BBC's *MasterChef* (although don't ask her to debone a rabbit; she has been a pescatarian for many years!).

Jennie is an ardent supporter of the charities Different Strokes and the Stroke Association after suffering a major stroke at the end of 2022. This profound moment led her to raise funds and awareness of strokes in younger people, as one in four strokes happen to people under the age of 60.

An experienced and passionate events host, Jennie shares her knowledge and love of F1 and women in motorsport with corporate clients and fans around the world.